Perihan Mağden is one of Turkey's most popular and innovative writers. She was born in Istanbul in 1960 and graduated from the Psychology Department at Istanbul's Bosphorous University. She has written novels, short stories and poems, and has lived in India and Japan. *The Messenger Boy Murders* is her first novel to be published in English. As well as her fiction and poetry, she writes a column for a leading Turkish newspaper.

Milet Publishing Ltd
6 North End Parade
London W14 0SJ
England
Email: orders@milet.com
Website: www.milet.com

The Messenger Boy Murders

First English edition published in 2003
by Milet Publishing Ltd

First published in Turkey as
Haberci Çocuk Cinayetleri in 1991

Copyright © Milet Publishing Ltd 2003

ISBN 1 84059 364 4

Printed and bound in Turkey

The
MESSENGER BOY MURDERS

Perihan Maǧden

Translated by
Richard Hamer

To
the
three
reasons
for
this
book:

My mother,

Serhan,

and

Fulya

The

MESSENGER BOY MURDERS

No One Has The Nerve

I was being kicked out of the Conservatory and the old dean had summoned me to his study to collect my misconduct report. "Believe me, my good sir," I told him, "it's not for my own sake that your decision dismays me. What concerns me is how the Conservatory will be able to shoulder the burden of having dismissed the most talented student ever to have passed through its doors – just for a couple of misdemeanours."

"I'm speechless," said the dean. "I've got nothing whatsoever to say to you."

My words "a couple of misdemeanours" must have made him think I was taking my bad behaviour lightly: I had caused a drunken uproar in the cafeteria, had driven the professor of Music History to a nervous breakdown, and had set fire to the school dormitory with kerosene. No wonder he didn't know what to say. But I was fed up with people who had nothing to say for themselves. I always knew what to say.

Naturally, a Conservatory student has every right to act as they wish, but causing an uproar in the cafeteria and burning down the dormitory are not small misdemeanours. But then, I wouldn't have done them if they were. What use was it, though, to argue over the extent of my rights with the old, white-haired dean? In a way I was fond of him. And no matter how hard he tried to hide it, I knew he also had a soft spot for me; though, since I'd worn his patience to the bone, he would never have admitted it.

Politely, I bade him farewell. My misconduct report in one hand, my purple velvet cloak and rough leather suitcase in the other, I made my way to the train station. After seven years away, I was returning home.

My father had died when I was young and as my mother was a touch eccentric, our house bore hardly any resemblance to the usual suffocating refuge of parental love – thank god! But it was still home, and I begrudged the idea of having to return there.

I got to the station just as my train was about to depart and I had to race down the platform searching out the number of my carriage. Out of breath, I climbed aboard only to find that I was sharing my compartment with a dwarf and his monkey.

The monkey was wearing a tight-fitting astrakhan coat and a matching kalpak-style hat. The dwarf was dressed in a wide-striped black gabardine suit and a wine-coloured satin waistcoat and was sporting a grey and vermilion striped silk tie. His tie-pin was a diamond the size of my thumbnail and his thick auburn hair was meticulously groomed back, emphasizing his disturbingly blue, sparkling eyes.

I stowed away my suitcase and cloak and sat down in the seat nearest the window. Allow me to admit that after such a miserable day, I was rather annoyed at having to share my journey with such a dolled-up dwarf and his monkey.

People with faults comfort me. I'm amused by their deficiencies and they remind me I'm not the only one who's less than perfect. Indeed, I would even go so far as to say that such people keep me going. But, if I'm totally honest, I can't be so enthusiastic about people with physical disabilities. Whenever I come across them, I get distressed and wonder why they don't just stay at home instead of venturing out and ruining my day. This dwarf, though, was a bundle of happiness. Instead of ashamedly covering up his physical fault-box, dressed in this irritatingly chic outfit, he was showing it off on this intercity train. Flushed with anger,

I couldn't help focusing on his cufflinks. One of them had the face of a Cheshire cat, set with diamonds and studded with emerald eyes. The other, a porcelain-faced little girl with a blond bob, was just like Alice in Wonderland.

"Yes," said the dwarf, "Alice. Alice in Wonderland."

The sound of his voice was astonishingly beautiful: soft, deep and slightly hoarse. It was impossible not to feel moved. I always think the sound of someone's voice is significant. I myself am a fine conversationalist but I have a horrible, high-pitched voice. This dwarf though: what a beautiful voice he had.

"Mmmm" I said, to give away as little as possible of my own voice. Besides, I do not automatically make friends with fellow travelling companions. Sudden intimacy with a person you have never met before is not my style.

"Let me introduce you," said the dwarf. "This is Isabelle!"

The monkey, or Isabelle rather, politely held out her hand. I offered mine, almost involuntarily, and took hold of her small, warm paw. I don't like shaking hands at all, especially with monkeys, but there was something about this dwarf's voice – an extraordinary politeness, charisma even, that charmed you into obeying him.

"Isabelle's not very well," said the dwarf. "Rather ill, actually."

As the gentleman spoke in that beautiful voice of his, Isabelle nodded sorrowfully. And when he finished his sentence she rolled her eyes and inclined her head to rest on his shoulder.

"There's a famous doctor with an excellent reputation in your town – which is why we are heading there. Otherwise, I agree with you absolutely: it doesn't give me a great deal of pleasure travelling about, exhibiting this ugly body of mine, distressing people with my appearance."

The train set off, and was moving about as slowly as it possibly could. Otherwise I would have opened the window and hurled myself out to split open my spoiled little head.

"Isabelle's quite taken by you," said the dwarf. "The moment she set eyes on you, heading towards us with that purple cloak and rough leather case in your hand, she prayed you would come and share our compartment."

"She must know some very short prayers," I said, "because I was running to catch the train. I was worried it would leave without me."

The dwarf — or the gentleman rather — smiled. He had the most beautiful smile I'd ever seen. Isabelle too had this well-mannered smile. What a dear monkey.

"I have just been kicked out of the Conservatory," I said, "but no doubt you'd guessed that. I'm going back home to my mother."

"Yes, I thought that must have been the case," said the dwarf. "If you fancy, we can slosh brandy all over your misconduct report and throw it out the window. It would help to get it off your mind: the Conservatory, music, and that city. No one should carry round in their head memories of a place they've just been expelled from."

Suddenly, I don't know why, but my eyes welled with tears and my voice trembled. "Just because I didn't write a happy end to a sad song," I said. "And I spoke my mind about all those sacred classical works. There were a couple of misdemeanours I'd committed as well, but you can't be thrown out of a place just for that!"

"Call it a coincidence," said the dwarf, "but I happen to have on me some of the most wonderful cognac. Let's have a drink and talk about something different."

We sloshed some brandy over my report, threw it out the window and changed the subject. Before long, my head was spinning and I'd dropped into a drunken stupor. When I opened my eyes again, we were stopped in front of a large station. Isabelle was sleeping soundly under a mink throw. The gentleman, on the other hand, was sitting bolt upright, fixing me with his shining eyes.

"You slept for hours," he said. "Isabelle, too. She's so overjoyed at meeting you, she hasn't had a single nightmare. She has this recurring incubus about death, you see. Isabelle is terrified of dying." There, he stopped and his eyes stared straight ahead. "Actually, she is dying," he said. "My only love is about to die and she is terrified of it. If only I could at least get her to conquer that fear. There's nothing to fear about dying. Not only will she be left alone, but I too."

He couldn't bring himself to complete his sentence. Those huge, slightly wild, sparkling blue eyes were staring out of the carriage window. Willingly or not, I too stared out of the window, at the crowds of people on the platform. What on earth was going on?

A knot of half a dozen bizarrely dressed characters surrounded an unbelievably handsome dark young man with black, shoulder-length hair. He was wearing a long, flowing white robe which reached down as far as his sandaled feet. His eyes seemed to herald the existence of other worlds, and in his hand he clutched what looked like a peacock feather which he gently waved back and forth. I looked closer and discovered that what I thought had been a feather was actually nothing of the sort. Instead, it was an old book, bound in black. The sight of him took my breath away and I could feel my heart pounding in my chest.

"The Prince of Manchuria," explained the gentleman-dwarf, "who some believe to be the New Messiah."

"The Prince of Manchuria!" I exclaimed.

The Prince and his entourage got onto the train and entered the compartment adjacent to ours.

"Manchuria is a very poor country," said the gentleman-dwarf. "He's a prince alright, but when the English came upon him, he was wallowing in filth and playing marbles with his friends in a muddy street. The moment the English saw him they cheered: 'Here is what we've been searching for! Here is the New Messiah.' It was his handsome features, his ethereal beauty that apparently convinced them. With lightening speed they kidnapped him and smuggled him out of Manchuria. His mother was by all accounts some boozy Irish anthropologist who had lived for years in Manchuria. She died giving birth to him. And apparently she had six toes on her right foot! Of all the things I know about her! I'm telling you all of this just as it was told to me. The English put him in solitary confinement in the hope of preserving his other-worldliness. And as you can gather from the expression on his face, the New Messiah, the Manchurian Prince, doesn't love people. Indeed, he is incapable of loving them. And when you come to think of all the hardships that Jesus went through just to be able to love mankind, you can't help feeling he's right. The other strange thing is the extent to which the English went to protect his body, which they once subjected to so much ill-treatment on its supposed path to enlightenment. That's as much as I know — though I doubt there's anyone who knows any more."

While the dwarf was recounting all this, Isabelle had woken up. She had started drawing pictures in the air with her forefinger. She had taken off her kalpak and now I could see her head more easily. There was a deep scar on her forehead and hanging from one of her ears was a butterfly-shaped earring set with diamonds.

The dwarf burst into one of his beautiful laughs. "Beloved Isabelle," he said, his eyes radiating love for her, "there's absolutely nothing you forget, is there?"

Isabelle smiled as she went on drawing circles in the air.

"Isabelle is reminding me of another detail I forgot to mention," explained the dwarf. "The English wanted the Manchurian Prince — who according to some is the New Messiah — to be given a classical education. He was given three years' private tuition by the very best teachers around to get him into Oxford. Then he went and caused a huge fiasco in the entrance exam. For the whole three hours he did nothing but doodle pictures of snails which resembled nothing other than the scribblings of an anxious five-year-old. When they told us this story Isabelle laughed so much she almost fell out of her armchair."

Isabelle smiled sweetly. It was obvious she was ill; she was but a shadow of the days when she could apparently laugh herself off her seat.

"I love Isabelle's earring," I said. "Just as I couldn't help noticing your cufflinks and tie-pin. Believe me, I've never seen such fine jewellery before."

And as soon as I'd said that, I turned beetroot red from head to toe. The more I tried not to be tactless, the more tactless I became. But I suppose that's life, isn't it? Don't we always get caught by what we are running away from?

Isabelle and the gentleman shook with laughter. Then, wiping the tears from his eyes with his purple silk handkerchief, the dwarf said, "Oh, you are so tactless! That's what makes you so charming, so entertaining. Even before a thought crosses your mind, it slips from your tongue. You're so charming, really, so charming."

Isabelle's laugh wasn't exactly a chuckle, but more a sort of painful growl that I was sure was ruining her liver. But I kept the thought to myself.

"All this precious jewellery is a part of my job," said the dwarf. "The more valuable jewellery one wears, the more one receives as gifts from one's clients. Perhaps we should say they are forced into competition and feel compelled to give it to you. My dear travelling companion, just as money begets money, jewellery invites more jewellery. Besides, it's a good investment, takes up little space, is easy to carry and can be cashed wherever you find yourself."

"Mmmm," I said again, but my voice sounded hoarse. What on earth could this gallant dwarf's profession be for him to receive so many valuable presents?

I was just in the process of thinking this when there was a polite knock on our compartment door.

"Come in," said the dwarf. "Come in."

It was one of the outlandishly attired Englishmen from the Manchurian Prince's entourage. He was a tall man with a beak-shaped nose and sandy hair and a smile like frozen butter – that typical forced English smile; that stiff upper lip, which makes you think 'ugh, why do they do that?' But in his hand he carried a basket of the most luscious figs and with his long arms he placed the basket beside me.

"For your mother, from His Majesty the Messiah," he said with an Oxbridge accent and an Oxbridge tone of voice. "His Majesty the Messiah, not wishing to disturb you, asked me to pass on a message: Your mother . . . "

"Yes, I know. My mother adores figs," I cut him short. "You may extend my deepest thanks to His Majesty of Manchuria . . . uhhh, Messiah. On behalf of my mother, of course."

Trying to get himself out of such deep water, the Englishman turned his steely eyes towards Isabelle. "Oh, what a sweet little monkey." And he reached out his hand to stroke her.

"Keep your hands off her!" I barked. "Don't touch Isabelle, sir. Besides, let's not keep you any longer – thanks for my mother's figs and have a good day."

I sounded so blunt, so rude, that the Englishman must have wondered what he had walked in on. With excuses like "ohhhh, errrr, ahhhhh" he saluted us all and left.

A quick exchange of glances between the dwarf and Isabelle was enough to set them off laughing again.

"What a nerve you've got!" said the dwarf. "You're one of a dying breed – no one has a nerve like yours anymore."

I inclined my head slightly. I liked Isabelle and the dwarf, and I took pleasure from being liked by them.

"Isabelle hasn't laughed so much in months," said the dwarf. "That's why I'm so grateful to you."

He held Isabelle's hand. Isabelle nodded touchingly as if to say, "Yes darling, you're right."

The two were in love with one another. Quite literally head over heels in love. How moving it was to observe, I thought. It had been months, years even since I had seen two people, two things, a person and a thing or whatever, so obviously in love.

"Your mother must be someone special," said the dwarf. "It is no small matter to be honoured by the Manchurian Prince, or, as some see him, the New Messiah. The poor child is engulfed by such loneliness; he views the world from behind a curtain of utter selfishness. As it is said in that favourite poem of mine — 'If the universe were to break into pieces one evening' — the young man would not even notice."

"You never know from under which stone my mother will emerge," I said. "I wouldn't know whether she is special or not. We don't see each other that often. She lives in the house my grandfather left her, along with her male-servant Wang Yu. And now I've spent so long away from home — at boarding schools and in travelling — that now I'm a stranger even to my hometown."

"I see," said the dwarf, using a phrase which people generally use when they don't see anything. But the dwarf, I think, had understood completely.

Isabelle must have been feeling hot, as she took off her astrakhan coat. Around her neck she wore a beautiful necklace — a companion piece to the butterfly earring, set with rubies, sapphires, diamonds and emeralds.

And of course, the dwarf noticed how my eyes lit up.

"Isabelle's just mad about butterflies. A lady admirer of mine who knows my how much I love Isabelle had this necklace made for her in Burma. The stones are superb, the craftsmanship is second to none and Isabelle enjoys wearing it from time to time. What more can I say?"

"So, does all your jewellery come from lady admirers?" I asked him — and as I said it, I realised how my voice sounded like that of a peacock.

"My profession is simply a way of earning enough to make ends meet," said the dwarf. "Isabelle and I live on a large estate and if we rarely go out it's because it's just too expensive. My earnings only just keep us going as it is. As I said earlier, I have no choice but to accept, or rather, encourage such gifts. We've led a destitute life in the past and I suppose you could say that this passion for jewellery is a guard against having to return there. In my profession, the moment I am no longer perfect, I will be forced to quit. And these jewels will ensure we are still able to live comfortably."

"Excuse me for asking . . . but if you don't mind . . . I mean, if I don't ask, then I'll burst — but what exactly is your profession?" I spluttered.

"Ahhh, I thought you'd understood that ages ago," he said flashing one of those beautiful smiles. "I am a gigolo."

"What?! . . . But with a body like that?!" I bawled out. I hadn't meant to be so rude.

"You mean, just because I'm a dwarf?" he said. "But that's my trump card."

"Your what? You mean, because you're a dwarf?" I garbled. Seeing my surprise, Isabelle was unable to contain her laughter.

"Yes," said the dwarf. "Forget about the psychological theory which claims that women seek lovers who resemble their fathers. Rather, they seek those who resemble their children — especially their as yet unborn children. And that's why being a dwarf is so important. I am not their superior; I'm not even their equal. But that, you see, is so plain that I don't delude myself — like so many other men – into thinking of myself as their superior. It's just so obvious I'm deficient – from head to toe, inside and out! So women can feel as much pity as they want towards me, make me the object of their desire and shower me with all their bottled-up passion. I'm the total opposite of all those brainless, heartless, able-bodied men who are utterly unable to satisfy a woman. I work only for money, and they know that I'll never love, wouldn't love, any of them. I don't pretend I will make a place in my heart for them. So I can't delude them, because I can't delude myself. They know that I only love Isabelle, but I do my job perfectly. They accept me as I am and that in itself is a great relief for them. Women either poison their life by trying to change a man they can't accept as he is, or as they feel some incredible love which is not reciprocated – such as for their children. When they are making love to me they taste the deepest, most overwhelming, inescapable of pleasures: the pleasure of incest. It's complicated, yet at the same time very simple. I have never tried to explain it to anyone before. I don't know if it made any sense to you."

I was shaking my head in wonder, like a child bending down to look in a well and seeing hundreds of stars in its depth, when I heard a racket outside our compartment.

A young man was screaming, "I want to talk! Leave me alone, I want to meet them! I want to speak with them."

Two or three other people were whispering to him to try to calm him down and persuade him to return to his compartment. I recognised one of the voices. It was the tedious Oxford graduate who had earlier brought us the figs. Then the talking stopped and the door of the adjacent compartment was slammed violently shut.

"The Manchurian Prince," said the dwarf, indicating the next-door compartment with his eyes. "He wanted to speak with us." He sighed deeply. "Ahh, poor young man! They don't even let him breathe, and then they expect from him philosophies to save the world . . . Believe me, nothing comes from a sterile environment: peace and quiet, isolation . . . or else the greatest philosopher of the twentieth century would have been Rudolph Hess!"

"Exactly!" I agreed. "Either him or Howard Hughes."

"When he was twelve the New Messiah wrote a marvellous book. Then, for the next seven years he didn't write a line. What could he experience while surrounded by those coffin-bearers? What could he feel? What could he write? Whatever I myself have learned about life, I learned in the circus where I was born. And together with Isabelle's love, it amounts to everything I know."

He turned and looked lovingly at Isabelle. Isabelle nodded coyly.

"So you were born in a circus?" I asked him.

"Yes," he answered. "I'm the son of a clown, himself a dwarf. My mother was the world's most beautiful acrobat. It's one thing I share with the Manchurian Prince that both of our mothers died in childbirth. Imagine how insufferable it would have been for such a beautiful woman to be the mother of a dwarf like me. When I was a child I tried to convince myself it was a good thing my mother had died by reflecting on this very thought. My father had been so besotted by my mother that he couldn't even bear to look at me and soon left for another circus. Then, three or four years later he fell from a trapeze and died — one of those deaths which is a mixture of accident and suicide. I was brought up by the circus cook: a big, fat and lonely lady who loved me enormously. Isabelle was the daughter of the most famous of the circus's monkeys. She was a frail, feeble baby and you can guess what happened . . . "

"Her mother died giving birth to her, too," I answered mischievously.

"Yes, that's exactly what happened," said the dwarf. "Monkeys are just like people, they need mothering, but the other monkeys didn't look after Isabelle. That frail, tiny thing. So sweet, so beautiful. It was me who brought her up, me who gave her a name, and taught her everything she knows. And in return,

Isabelle has made me happy."

He turned and gazed at Isabelle for a long time. She had once again crept beneath her mink throw, and was sleeping heavily.

"I've tired you out," he said, with heart-winning politeness. "Look, you're sleepy."

Our compartment was warm. Outside it was dark and we were passing through a forest. I was overcome by sleep.

When I awoke the train was just drawing into the station at my hometown. Isabelle and the dwarf had gone, and I felt upset not to have said goodbye. Then, I noticed on the basket of figs, an envelope with my name written in exquisitely beautiful handwriting. I opened it and on a sheet of beige-coloured parchment was a letter:

> *Our dear, dear travelling companion,*
>
> *You made Isabelle and myself so happy that . . . when Isabelle woke up she was completely recovered. Your liveliness, your youth, your courage towards life changed her. Now there is no need to visit the doctor in your town; indeed Isabelle doesn't even need to see a doctor at all. Her desire is to pass her last days in peace and happiness at our home. We are fortunate indeed to have met you.*
>
> *It's only a small keepsake, but I hope you will accept it. Maybe you can sell it and the money will finance new adventures. What do you think?*

His signature was eye-catching. There was something special, unique about it, yet it was totally illegible. In the envelope was his tie-pin with its diamond the size of my thumbnail. I placed it in the palm of my hand and stared at it. It held the promise of future travels – to India, Nepal, Sri Lanka, Burma . . .

But my present journey had just come to an end. 🐚

THE SECRET MEANINGS OF UNAPPRECIATED WORDS

Back then I was working at the paper factory, though I was ignored by the rest of the factory workers. Maybe because I always wore black, or because I'd been to such places as Singapore or because I ate my mother's tasteless meatloaf sandwiches instead of factory rations at lunchtime. I was so lonely and fed up that I longed for them to recognise my existence just so that I could be obnoxious back to them. I would have belittled them without their realizing it and a couple of weeks later, when it had finally dawned on them what I had said, they would have gone into a frenzy. But instead, flock-like, they kept their distance and except for giggling over the aphorisms I would occasionally toss at them, they refused to have anything to do with me. As I just explained, I was going through a particularly rough patch at the time and I was just too lazy to mix with them. Instead, I went round like a poor, lonely wolf among a pack of Little Red Riding Hoods.

It was this sense of isolation that drove me to write my dictionary: *The Real Meanings of Certain Unappreciated Words*. I have succeeded in infiltrating some of the most secret societies all over the world, but I would never have survived the night I am about to narrate if the obstinacy of the workers in the paper factory had not pushed me to write that dictionary. So, in a way, I suppose I ought to be grateful to them.

Just like every other day, when the bell rang to signal the end of the shift, everyone rushed to the doors. Only I was in no hurry. I had no one to meet and nothing to do other than to go back home to my dictionary, and I was chewing over how I would rewrite some sentence or other. The five o'clock bell just served to remind me how busy they all were — and how respectively empty my own life was.

I came to the factory gates and gazed at the statues of Icarus and Pegasus that perched on each of the gateposts. Those two winged statues rising above their respective white pillars were perhaps the only reason why I had wanted to work at the paper factory. The monotony of the work, the bells, the rules, the feeling of being part of the machine and the insidious pleasure of watching the other workers were, in fact, all responsible for my spending more time there than I might ever have imagined. But the factory gate was where it all ended. As soon as I passed through its opening, I quickened my stride and walked as if I was late for something.

But on this particular evening, I couldn't bear the thought of facing either my mother's venomous cooking or of the painful hours at my desk extracting the meaning of some unappreciated word and constructing a definition. I turned down a side street. Then another. Right in front of me, with its steamed-up window, was the restaurant. It was one of those places frequented by single male factory workers, but, nevertheless, I pushed open the door and entered . . .

The next day, beneath the souvenir of a terrible hangover bestowed on me by all the red wine, I could recall only fragments of that evening. It happens every time I drink too much, too quickly and, now, as I recount the events of the evening, you should bear in mind that there may be things I've forgotten. On the other hand, there may well be things I've imagined. But, with this headache of mine, what does it matter? Just don't expect too much of me.

I had sat down at a small square table in a hidden corner. Contrary to my usual habit of ordering kidneys or pork chops,

I remember ordering a meat dish with carrots or peas, and after eating the meat, playing a sort of philosophical chess game by myself with the peas versus the carrots. Only, I was downing the dry red wine so fast that I can't remember the details of the game. I can only vaguely recall that the peas were pure while the carrots were corrupt.

I'm not one of those people who can keep themselves occupied for long. As I drained the wine in my glass, I lifted my head and shouted at the restaurant owner: "Sabartés! Sabartés, another jug of red wine!"

The restaurant owner was a man of experience; not one of those types who keep pestering you to explain what you mean. Rotten-hearted people like myself who feel licensed to behave just as they feel, immediately sense how easy some people are to pester. Even in my half-drunken stupor, I could tell what a good soul the restaurant owner was. He could even put up with me calling him by a Catalan name!

Sabartés had just left another jug of wine on my table when the door opened and a broad-shouldered dwarf walked in. Since my childhood I have never been able to keep my eyes off a dwarf when I see one. Years ago, I came across a dwarf while travelling in Peshawar. He noticed my eyes crawling like snakes all over him, and, as if to punish me, he screwed up his face, madly swung his arms about, and turned somersaults. But then, that's the kind of behaviour you'd expect from a dwarf, isn't it?

It makes my hair stand on end just to recall this episode, but it still didn't stop me staring at the dwarf who had just walked through the door as if I was watching a skyscraper on fire. The strangest thing about this dwarf was that he was rather tall. If he ever placed an ad in the Lonely Hearts section of a dwarf newspaper, he would have been quite justified in describing himself as 'tall, broad-shouldered'. Two dignified gentlemen sitting at the table opposite me greeted him warmly — it was clear that people felt great affection for this dwarf. But he was still a dwarf!

I was so absorbed that I didn't notice that someone had sat down on the chair next to me – or at least, not until he turned to fix his eyes on me. I guess in this restaurant it was quite acceptable to just sit down at someone else's table without asking their permission. "Aren't you the author of *The Secret Meanings of Unappreciated Words*?" he asked with a smoker's rasp in his voice.

Slightly misquoting the title, he had omitted the word 'certain' and replaced the word 'real' with 'secret'. But I had to agree that his title sounded more accurate, more pleasant even. I was taken aback.

"Why don't you sit opposite me?" I suggested. "Then I can see your face more easily."

He got up, moved to the chair directly opposite, and sat down again. He was a dark, beautiful man with dirty, slicked-back hair and glaring eyes. His upper lip was conspicuously thinner than his lower lip, which gave him a covetous kind of expression. He spoke with a fast stutter – the kind of voice you wouldn't expect from a smoker. Moreover, I remember he had long, slender hands. Because my own fingers are so stumpy, I always try to be respectful towards people with slender hands.

I pulled over the wine jug and reached for his glass. "I hope you wouldn't say no to a glass of wine."

He smiled and nodded his approval. Actually, it wasn't a real, heart-felt smile, since he was one of those people who don't have a spontaneous smile. I filled up his glass and just as I was putting it down in front of him, Sabartés came over to our table. He handed each of us a pair of wool stockings.

"It's a custom in this restaurant," explained the stranger. "Anyone whose feet feel cold gets a pair of wool stockings."

"I've only got tonight to get used to the customs of this restaurant," I told him. "Tomorrow I am setting out on a long journey."

"So you're quitting your job at the paper factory," said the man.

"I've never cared about that job."

He narrowed his eyes, and once again pursed his lips into that semi-smile. He understood that neither this, nor any other job was ever important to me. "How do you know?" I asked.

"I paid the price to find out," he said.

"The price?" I said. No one is better than me at meaningless chatter — I can talk for hours about nothing in particular, but I am struck dumb whenever someone says something profound.

"You are a traveller," said the man. "You're forever setting out on the road."

"You seem incapable of smiling," I interjected. "Is that the price you paid?"

I can never keep my mouth shut! One of these days I will drop dead from the shame this illness brings me. I turned bright red and stared at the floor. I was so ashamed of what I'd just said that I couldn't sit at the same table with him any longer. I leapt up from my chair and a moment later was sitting down at the table with the dwarf and the two gentlemen.

"May I join you?" I asked. "Right at this moment, I'm in need of shelter."

"With pleasure," said the man with blue eyes. With his blond, greying hair and thick neck, he was a veritable lion of a man.

"Geishas speak of music, politics and poetry," I said. "What would you like me to talk about?"

"What we were just talking about was interesting," said the dwarf.

This was more than I could stand. I was fed up with dwarves giving me lessons on life. I called Sabartés and ordered a crème caramel.

"Please forgive my brother," said the lion of a man. "He can be extremely outspoken."

"Your brother?!" I exclaimed. "A dwarf and a lion!"

"You said it so beautifully!" said the dwarf as he burst out laughing. "Is your name, by any chance, Sheherazade?"

I only just managed to restrain myself from saying that *he* was more like the one from a fairy tale.

"If you say so, sir," I said instead. "But now, if you don't mind, I would like to eat my dessert."

Crème caramel alone, though, was not enough to relieve my despondency. I called Sabartés over once more and asked him to bring me a potato salad. I like eating a desert when I am distressed, but I like to follow it with something salty. The dwarf and the other two plunged into a deep conversation, discussing Burma, the price of lapis, giraffes, and other such things. The dark stranger was finishing off a plate of pork chops and trying not to make it too obvious, I observed him carefully.

While collecting his empty plate from in front of him, Sabartés commented, "What a wonder, sir! Don't you usually order the casserole and play a sort of chess game with the peas and carrots?"

"Tonight is different, Sabartés," said the beautiful man.

'Sabartés'?! Hadn't I been the one to give him that nickname? The man paid his bill, got up from the table and left. He'd stolen half my heart — and made me want to sink the other rotten half into a river to cleanse it.

Or at least that was how I felt for five minutes, until the second gentleman (the lion of a man, the friend of the brother of the tall dwarf) said: "Don't be upset. He was only trying to change you. Those kinds of people show you affection, but you have to be aware it's not disinterested or limitless. They show you a small touch of fondness and in return, they expect you to change to suit them. Not that you might be any better or worse, but just that you become moulded by them."

"You're quite right. I'm pleased to have met you," I said.

"Well, at least my heartache lasted only five minutes."

"Sometimes it can last five weeks, or five thousand hours, or even five years," said the man. "Mine, alas, lasted even longer. Do you see my eye? This right eye of mine?"

"Yes, it's artificial, isn't it?" I said. You could hardly fail to notice it. His left eye was brown, but his right eye was blue and glistened like a glass bead. He had sparse sandy hair and a thin, flat nose. Actually, he was a fine man, and very well dressed. If you passed him in the street you would have guessed him to be a Harvard anthropology graduate — or at worst, a Columbia anthropology graduate.

"I lost it during the war," he said. "I was sitting at the dinner table along with my beautiful wife and our two children. We were eating soup, when all of a sudden I felt I was swimming in the soup bowl. It was terrifying. It was impossible for me to get out of the bowl. And what's more," said the gentleman with the artificial eye, "I still continue to live quite normally at my home with my wife and children. I just don't go home for dinner, that's all."

I tried to say things such as 'I see', 'I understand', but I was so shaken that all I really wanted to do was to run away. My head was going round in circles and, excusing myself politely, I told them that I should return to my table.

"Yes, perhaps you'd better," said the Harvard graduate with the glass eye. "And also, you have an interesting new guest. Mr. Elya will be ordained a rabbi in two weeks. And what's more, he is a convert — he became a Jew with his own sweat and blood. He left the Music Academy in order to walk through the labyrinths of religion. Tonight the stars are shining for you!"

"Thank you, gentlemen," I stuttered. "Good night."

"I heard that you have been walking through the labyrinths of religion," I said to the newcomer at my table. "What's more, you left the Music Academy which cost you so much effort to get into. I'm afraid you might be the type who walks away from everything. But, I must admit, your yarmulke looks good on you. Do you take it off when you go to bed?"

"There is nothing in life that can't be left behind," said Mister Elya. "We exist in a world where the value of something is proportional to how easy it is to leave behind. Otherwise, our existence on this earthly world is confined to a prison yard. Don't misunderstand me, by leaving something behind, we not only widen that prison yard, but we also define our status when we eventually meet our deaths."

"Don't be afraid of my not understanding you, Mr. Elya," I said. "Because I do not understand you at all."

"Actually, the prison wardens would see your vulgarity as a threat," he said. "And please, how about leaving the 'Mister' aside. My name is Elya, just Elya."

"I understand, sir," I said. This phrase was turning out to be my lifesaver. It came out of my mouth the moment I'd understood even the slightest trace of what was being said. I filled up his empty glass and as he took his first sips, I eyed him carefully. He had curly, fluffy hair and green eyes with long lashes. His skin was so pale it was almost transparent – like that of everyone who takes up religion. It's probably a little gift for distancing oneself from the workings of the world. He was wearing a dark green shirt of which the top three buttons were left undone to reveal a black T-shirt with the word 'First' printed on it.

"I can guess what is written on the T-shirt," I said. "They probably sell them at the synagogue. Is yours a special print for the rabbis? Yes, I'm positive. It says: 'First There Was The Word'.

He smiled a soft, forgiving, almost luminous smile which seemed to light up our table and the surrounding tables. The Harvard gentleman blinked and Elya slowly unbuttoned his shirt. Written on his T-shirt was the slogan:

First
There Were
The Rolling
Stones

"Nobody would believe me if I told them what happened here tonight," I said.

"You are taking everything personally," said Elya.

I was thinking about that handsome dark man again. Besides, I had no more strength to counter Elya. "How beautifully you put it," I said. "How beautifully you put it."

Just at that moment the dwarf sprang up by our table. His eyes were directed at Elya and gleaming with love. So, he wasn't only a dwarf who inspired affection, but a loving one as well. It was obvious from their manner they had much to say to each other.

I got up slowly, went over to Sabartés and asked for my bill. "Your bill has been taken care of," Sabartés said. Reaching for the first drawer of the counter behind him, he pulled out a red rose with a long stem. "And also, he left this for you."

"Good evening, Sabartés," I said. "Thank you for the stockings."

He was a man of dignity indeed. There was no need to exaggerate. I took up the rose and left the restaurant.

It was late and there was no one about. Walking along, I picked the rose petals and crushed them in my fingers. I snapped the stem into pieces as I wound my way through the winding streets back home. At home all the lights were out. My mother must have gone to bed a long time ago.

I went into my room and turned on the lamp on top of the dresser. A shaky light lit up the shadows. My rough leather suitcase was in its usual place, lying under my bed like a loyal dog and I pulled it out to place it on my bed. I packed my blue-covered notebook, my three books, my soap dish, my little pillow and a few pieces of clothing. I like living off whatever I can find in the places I go to. Travelling with too much luggage is for people who don't know how to travel.

I sat on one of the chairs at the round mahogany table in the middle of the room and wrote out my resignation from the paper factory. Then, I started emptying the pockets of my jacket — which is something I do every night before going to bed.

In the right pocket (which I usually leave empty) I found a ticket, a rose stem and a handkerchief. My keys and the coins were in my left pocket and I put the whole lot down on the table-top. A gleaming blue glass bead rolled out from among the coins. I picked it up and looked at it. This was more than I could take! I tossed it back onto the table, then picked up my pen and started to write on a sheet of parchment:

Very Deserving Sabartés,

> *I think this artificial eye that I found in my left pocket belongs to the gentleman from Harvard who is the friend of the lion-man — the dwarf's brother. I've no idea how it ended up in my pocket. I suppose we could just put it down to one of the many inexplicable things that happened this evening. I beg you to return the eye to its owner as soon as possible. Ever grateful for all your help . . .*

I signed the letter and placed it in an envelope along with the eye. As I sealed the envelope, I felt as if some great weight had been taken off my shoulders. Believe me, it's not easy to get rid of an artificial eye that has somehow found its way into your pocket.

Straight away I called one of the twenty-four hour private messenger centres. Five minutes later, a messenger boy rang the bell. Like all the messenger boys of this city, he had curly blonde hair, pure blue eyes and dimples. And also, like all the other messenger boys, he wore yellow and lilac striped velvet breeches, white stockings with pompoms, patent leather shoes with bows, and on top, a short jacket of the same lilac velvet and finished off with a starched white lace on the collar and the cuffs.

"You can deliver this letter to the paper factory in the morning," I said. "And take this envelope to a restaurant with a steamed-up plate glass window. I suspect the name of the restaurant owner is Sabartés. Or rather, I'm sure it is."

"I understand," he said.

"Good night, messenger boy," I said.

"Good night," he said.

He went out – and disappeared with fast, silent steps.

The messenger Boy Murders

I returned home after a long journey to find a black cloud hanging over the city, but it was an unspoken rule for the townspeople never to discuss evil happenings. If something was going wrong, everyone waited patiently until the evil ended before they would talk about it. I could never understand, though, their quiet belief in fending off evil with silence. But then, there were so many incorrigible things in this city that I had given up trying to understand them long ago. So, on this occasion, even if someone had bluntly alluded to recent events, I doubt if I'd have bothered to worry about it. I was tired, and like every other time I came home from a long journey, all I wanted to do was sleep. I shut myself in my room and the days flowed by like a heavy, muddy river. I slept for weeks and didn't come round until the first days of spring. I was even more tired than when I'd returned, but I was driven out of the house with the same enduring fear that if I didn't get out and about, I never would.

My legs trembled and, as I walked, every one of my muscles hurt. One street ran into another and I had no idea where I was going, until, at length, I found myself in front of the old green wooden door of Monsieur Jacob's bookshop. Every time I came back to the city I found myself in front of that duck-green door, and every time it made me happy.

Years ago, someone carved *Moi aussi* on the door with a knife. Monsieur Jacob yelled until he frothed at the mouth, and, with flashing eyes, swore that he'd buy a new door, and then inscribe on it a word I'd be too embarrassed to mention here. That line on the door was so meaningful, however, the blade so skilled, that before long, Monsieur Jacob and his customers began to like the shop ever more for it. Moi aussi.

No matter how pleased I was at seeing Monsieur Jacob, we both greeted each other a little distantly. The inhabitants of my city embrace each other with such joy that it brings a shine to the eyes; but somehow, I always feel awkward greeting and saying goodbye to people.

Fortunately, Monsieur Jacob wasn't put out (he wasn't a native of the city and had moved here when he was forty) – and as a matter of fact, in a lively tone, he said "Don't I just know what you're looking for? You're after one of those horse trainer biographies again."

One couldn't say I had an addictive personality, but I am extremely fond of biographies, especially seven-volume horse trainer biographies. "Exactly, Monsieur Jacob," I said. "Believe me, at this particular moment, I'm ready to give up three weeks of sleep for a long, involved biography."

"Aaah, ah!" said Monsieur Jacob regretfully. "I had just the book for you. But, one of my new customers – a fairly nondescript character – 'Mr. Wolfscientist' I call him . . . It had been there three or four days when, last Wednesday, he bought just the horse trainer biography you are looking for. When he next drops by, I'll send him in your direction so you can get the book from him."

I interrupted angrily: "Who is this 'Mr. Wolfscientist'? What rotten times we live in! Would I go out and buy books on the courtship patterns of wolves? Believe me, Monsieur Jacob, I just loathe this era of everyone being interested in everything."

In fact, I also loathed Monsieur Jacob for daring to sell such a rare volume to Mr. Wolfscientist at the hour of my greatest need.

"Don't ask," said Monsieur Jacob. "Don't. Everyone is into everything nowadays. The other day an engineer bought himself a book on ballet bound in pink. And a jeweller, on a whim, bought one of my rarest historical atlases! I doubt whether he can even read or write — but book-buying has come into fashion."

"Tell me exactly who this Mr. Wolfscientist is," I hissed. "If he doesn't have a name, surely he has a body."

"Believe me, he has neither a memorable name nor a note-worthy appearance," said Monsieur Jacob. "Just a profound knowledge of wolves — to which he has devoted so many years of study. But now, it seems, he works as a stockbroker in order to make a living. Such a well-mannered, but inconsequential man. Don't press me further."

I was looking at him with such hatred that he began to sweat great beads. "Alright, Monsieur Jacob," I said. "I don't want to upset you over a miserable biography. But I'd be much obliged if you would get those seven volumes to me. Especially seeing as I've just come back from my travels . . . "

"Ah, ah, ah!" said Monsieur Jacob. Riven with guilt, his old eyes glowed like coals with the desire to win back my heart. "I wonder if you've noticed anything strange about the city?"

"How could I not notice, Monsieur Jacob?" I said. "You could cut this city's silence with a knife."

"Messenger boy murders," he whispered. "They are being murdered one by one. Nobody can explain why."

"Messenger boy murders!" I exclaimed so loudly that all of a sudden a book from one of the top shelves fell on my head. I put the book on the counter and my eyes were inadvertently drawn to the title: *Wolves: Changing mating patterns under ecological pressure.*

In this city where there were at most three murders a year, to hear of serial murder — moreover of messenger boy murder — was no trifling matter. If Monsieur Jacob's intention had been to win my heart and appease my fury by broaching such an unmentionable subject, I must say he had succeeded. Almost stuttering with surprise, I said, "For goodness sake, Monsieur Jacob, do you know what you're saying?"

"I'm absolutely aware," he winked. "I'd been meaning to talk to you about it. If anyone can solve this case, you can. You're both a native and a foreigner to this town. This is your hometown, yet if anything goes wrong, you're immediately off to foreign shores. That is to say that you are both part of this city and completely outside of it – you are our only hope."

"Our only hope?" I asked, astonished. "Have you discussed this matter with the townspeople? Monsieur Jacob, in this town nobody speaks about evil happenings – which no doubt accounts for the abundance of silence in the town."

"Believe me, this time it's different," said old Jacob. "This time the situation is grave. Even if we don't want to, we're talking. Silence is no longer possible. The more we cover it with silence, the louder it shouts." With tears in his eyes and his voice cracking, he said, "They are being killed one by one."

He started to sob. This was the first time I'd ever seen anyone in that city cry. If I have a soft spot at all in my stony heart, then it belongs to the elderly. The perpetual games of their childish spirit are, for me, like the most beautiful seashells scattered over the shores of wisdom. Seeing Jacob's tears, my limbs went numb and my throat tightened. With tears in my eyes I said, "Please, Monsieur Jacob." I spoke with difficulty, my throat hurt. "I beg you to calm down."

That clever Jacob! It was as though his tears were intended to move me and to make me say those words. He wiped his eyes with the back of his hand. "Ah, so you'll help us then, won't you?" he said in an almost merry, triumphant manner.

"Monsieur Jacob, you know I'm a recluse," I stuttered. "Are you aware of how much I would have to give of myself to deal with this case and get to the bottom of it – let alone succeed?!"

"How could I not be aware?" Monsieur Jacob snapped back. "But, pray tell, who else could one have thought of for this matter besides you? You're intelligent, you're sceptical, you're savage, and being a recluse, you're free. You suffered in order to open up that eye on your forehead."

"Please, Monsieur Jacob," I said rubbing my forehead. "Please, it's time for me to go." My face was crimson, I could hardly stand. That Jacob could have tricked the devil into wearing his shoes on the wrong feet, even make the devil thank him for the favour.

"Whatever you wish," he said. "I knew from the beginning you would say yes."

"I'll think about it, Monsieur Jacob," I said. "I wouldn't count that as a yes, but I'll think about it. And, if you'll wrap this book up for me, who knows, maybe one day I'll make a gift of it to Mr. Wolfscientist . . . " With *Wolves: Changing mating patterns under ecological pressure* wrapped in shiny duck-green paper in hand, I returned home deep in thought.

That night, I lay down wanting to dive into a deep sleep and wake up the next morning in a bamboo hut by the ocean having completely forgotten about Jacob, the messenger boy murders, and the city. Instead, my head worked all night like a springless clock. Such crazy thoughts passed through my mind that, half-awake, half-asleep, I left myself to the flow and let the fantastic scenes pass in front of my eyes. I only fell asleep when the first rays of the day were licking the heavy velvet curtains of my room.

Perhaps I could have pulled myself together a bit if I had slept till the evening; perhaps I could have freed myself from the nightmarish state in which I found myself. However, towards noon I awoke to the heavy footsteps of my mother.

Even though she's a small woman, my mother moves briskly and noisily, making as much noise in the house as Hannibal's armies might have. When not engaged in this frantic rushing around, she orders Wang Yu about, criticizing everything he does — and the only way to escape from this overwhelming restlessness is to leave the house.

All I wanted was to be as tired, empty and carefree as when I had come back, to drown in the rivers of sleep. Jacob! Treacherous Jacob! Burning with anger at him for having involved me in that business, I got dressed and went downstairs.

Wang Yu, with his wonderfully insincere smile, said, "Good morning. An omelette? A tuna sandwich? Or both?"

"Tea, Wang Yu," I said. "Tea and both of them together."

Wang Yu was like a bad copy of my mother. He made as much noise as possible while preparing breakfast for his mistress's child, having turned his back and assumed the long-suffering and loyal servant pose. His whole life revolved around my mother. As for me, I was only tolerated as one of those liabilities that is the lot of all perfect servants. If I can't make out how and which unknown wind had blown that seven-times-cursed Indian servant with a Chinese name into our house, I know as well as I know my own name that he would never have set foot in any place other than my mother's home.

At first, Wang Yu hated my mother, but hating her, he learned her moods so well that in the end my mother's moods became his own. In this way Wang Yu split right down the middle: to the world he played my mother; while to my mother he went on acting like a thirteen-year-old. As a child, whenever he came to pick me up from school, I would die of embarrassment. As soon as the bell rang, I would streak out of class like an arrow and race home. Unperturbed, Wang Yu would follow in my trail as if it was only a prank, and later, he'd say, "My goodness! How could you do such a thing to Wang Yu?"

I pretended not to see him, behaved as if I wasn't aware of his existence, so that he was at peace to perform the duet with my mother. I suspect that this is exactly what Wang Yu wanted: to have no one else, particularly a migrant like me, involved in the love–hate, make-believe world he shared with my mother.

After finishing breakfast, I left Wang Yu to face his unending kitchen chores and went up to my grandfather's room. My grandfather had died nineteen years before, but nothing in the room had been touched. Everything had been preserved exactly as he'd left it one cold winter morning. According to my mother this was out of respect for her esteemed father, out of fondness for his memory and, above all, due to her being a sensitive soul. But I myself was sure that it was only out of apathy, and entirely attributable to the undisciplined and disorderly natures of my mother and Wang Yu.

I hadn't been in that room for quite some time. I looked at the first edition of *Moby Dick* on his bedside table, his worn out green leather slippers under the bed, his cigarette holders, dossiers and bulbous fountain pen left on the table, and my eyes filled with tears. Yesterday tears for Jacob, today for my grandfather! If I went on shedding tears for some old man every god-given day, I would get nowhere. Immediately I pulled myself together, assumed my usual rude, choleric countenance, and headed straight for my grandfather's wardrobe. The trench coat was just where it always was, hanging on the right side of the wardrobe. I took it off of the hanger, placed it on my shoulders, and stomped out of the room.

My grandfather always carried his keys in the left pocket of his trench coat. Even when he had drunk enough to forget which street his house was on, he never forgot where his keys were. So I wasn't at all surprised when thrusting my hand into the left pocket, to find his thick key-ring. The key-ring my grandfather had used all his life was extremely weird. He'd received it as a gift in Bombay, where he had spent his youth, and had once explained to me how it was a lucky charm. He'd promised to give it to me on my eighteenth birthday. Made of ivory, it was the head of

Murugan, one of the Hindu gods. This Murugan head, with its fanciful, optimistic expression and flawless peacock tail at the back of the head, was so intricately crafted that one couldn't stop admiring it. And the eyes were encrusted with two sapphire stones which looked almost satanic but which were also strangely compelling.

Fiddling with the key-ring I passed through the city's winding streets till I came to the old building where on the third floor was my grandfather's office. The bevel-edged copper sign on the door was completely covered with dust and the writing was illegible. I wiped it with the back of my hand. The letters

YAMIN   ROGIN   VOCATE

emerged. With the white handkerchief my mother had once embroidered with my initials, I wiped the sign. The words

BUNYAMIN STAVROGIN
ADVOCATE

came out in glory. I turned the lock and went in.

The room was full of dust and my grandfather's still lingering scent: a mixed perfume of old man, tobacco, liquor and lavender cologne. I opened the shutters to let in the daylight, but I did not want to disturb that peerless air of an undisturbed twenty years by opening the window. I crossed over to the head of my grandfather's massive oak desk and sat down in his revolving chair. I glanced around; there were movie magazines everywhere. There were movie magazines on top of and under the tables, on the filing cabinets, on the chairs. I opened the drawers of the desk. They contained every imaginable kind of paper and an assortment of whiskey bottles — some much-consumed, some hardly-touched, and others totally-unopened.

I opened one of the bottles. There was a glass right on the table, so I wiped it with rough paper and rinsed it with whiskey. My grandfather only drank whiskey at least twenty-one years old. I filled my glass, inhaled the magnificent scent of the whiskey, and set about drinking. I would tell Wang Yu to come the next morning to clean the place up, but I'd warn him never to open the windows.

I was afraid that I had been tricked by Jacob: my mind and spirit were devoted to the messenger boy murders. My head pounded with fatigue, my insides burned from nerves. I poured a little more whiskey in my emptied glass and took one of the movie magazines in hand, but it was so dusty that I hurled it back on the table. I stretched my feet out on the desk and fell into a deep sleep. I was free-falling through a bottomless well of sleep when all of a sudden there was a racket at the door. I found myself standing by the door without even being aware that I'd woken up. Someone was banging violently at the door and shouting, "Open up, please open up!" I opened the door and a man burst in. He was dressed in a short beige overcoat and an Irish hiking cap and was wearing a pair of round wire-framed spectacles. He was short and plump: a rather ridiculous man. Though I would realize quite how ridiculous he was only once he began talking, even at first glance, I could not refrain from wondering who this ridiculous man could be. I couldn't decide whether to call him Irish-Cap-Man or Mr. Ridiculous but in the end, I decided to call him Irish-Cap-Man. As for the matter of his being ridiculous or not, from this point on I leave that up to you.

"D-d-don't ask," the Irish-Cap-Man stuttered, while trying to wipe off the dust from the leather armchair to his right.

"Sir," I said. "Sir, why don't you use my handkerchief? This place has been gathering dust for twenty years."

He snatched my handkerchief and went at the armchair with it. Furiously wiping away the dust, stuttering and spluttering, he still managed to explain his business. "When I heard, I was so pleased. Very, very pleased. That means it's you. I know you from a distance. That is, from Mo-Monsieur Jacob's shop. I think he's r-right; only you can solve this case. What an ugly situation, so ugly, so ugly."

With all his effort he could only clear a tiny patch of dust from the armchair; then he suddenly collapsed in it and planted his eyes on mine. His eyes were dull and innocent: they seemed to resemble a dog's. I silenced him with my cold expression. Then I said in a fatherly, precise voice: "My good man. Please be calm. I'll not ask you who you are, how you found this place, or why you came – that is, nothing that would distress or disturb you. It's apparent you have something you want to tell me. I've got time, we're all alone; so, at your service: I'm listening."

Grabbing one of the movie magazines on the table, he said, "I don't look like him. No, I don't resemble him. But I too am in love with Lauren Bacall."

"Look, sir," I said in a voice crackling with rage. "I don't know how I've got myself into this business. I don't even know the details of this case, such as how many messenger boys there are in the city, how many of them have been murdered, or how and where they were murdered. Besides, I don't like numbers at all. Nor asking questions and striding through the streets . . . But you should understand that in spite of all this, I'm going to try to do something. As for your not resembling Bogart, you're absolutely right. But anyway, I hope you'll keep me company and accept a glass of whiskey. It'll do your nerves some good, too."

I filled my glass again and gulped it down. My stomach burned mercilessly. The Irish-Cap-Man started to laugh shakily.

"You won't b-b-believe it," he said, "but in the inside pocket of my overcoat there's a glass. I got it today. Just today I bought it. Look, what a coincidence!" He pulled out a little blue glass and handed it over. I filled it to the brim.

"Okay, sir," I said, "do you have any chocolate? If you've also bought some chocolate today and you're carrying it around in your breast pocket, I may actually start to like you. Yes, in spite of myself, I'm already starting to like you."

"That's what love is all about," he said bursting with laughter. "Everything else is only really the annoyance of equilateral triangles."

As he shook with laughter he had trouble holding onto the packet of chocolate that he had removed from the inside pocket of his overcoat and held out to me. We drank whiskey, ate chocolate, and discussed Lauren Bacall.

"Hell of a woman!" he exclaimed repeatedly until he blinked and concluded: "In spite of myself, I love her." He then repeated this phrase ten or fifteen times until the bottle of whiskey was finished. "Ah! The time!" he said as he hurled himself out of his seat. Trying to put on his overcoat, he mumbled, "I was going to pick up my mother, she'll be so angry with me." With his jerking movements, attempting to do so many things at once, he looked like a wind-up toy.

He was hurrying out the door in such a panic. "My good man," I said, "You forgot your glass."

"Please, leave it here," he said. "I didn't get to talk about any-thing that I wished to. She's such a hell of a woman, she can drive you crazy." Exploding with laughter he went down the stairs. I closed the door, crossed over to the armchair behind the table and fell into a deep sleep.

In my dream, a woman's hand in a red lace glove was tearing up a picture of one of the messenger boys. It didn't matter which messenger boy's picture it was because all the messenger boys in this city looked alike. They all had curly blond hair, brilliant blue eyes and dimples. With their identical features and uniforms, it was impossible to tell them apart. Their starched collars and cuffs never got dirty; no mud spattered them or spoiled their cleanliness and beauty. Walking with soft, swift steps they enchanted all with their elegance.

Back in my dream, a grief-stricken, abandoned Afghan hound wandered the empty streets of the city, wafting its half-shed hair. Just then, a messenger boy about to cross the road noticed it with loathing. The dog had two mouths, one on top of the other, and, longing for affection, was about to die from loneliness and old age. It crossed over the road, fixed its lovelorn eyes on the lovely messenger boy as if to say "love me, love me, love me", and began to rub imploringly. The messenger boy, horrified at the thought that his clean clothes might get dirty, wished it would drop dead instantly. No one touched messenger boys. They remained virgins till the end of their lives; they abhorred all forms of physical contact. There, at that moment, a woman's hand in a red lace glove began tearing the messenger boy apart. In hair-raising screams she shouted, "Merciless! Merciless!"

I woke up in a sweat. It was long past midnight. I immediately left the office and ran straight for home. I was immersed in an incredible, uncomprehending fear. It was as if the city stank of murder. Just as I made it to the front of my home someone gently crept up behind me and struck me on the head with a hard object. Next morning, when I came to, I could have sworn the hand that struck me was covered in a red lace glove.

<hr />

Wearing his superficial smile Wang Yu came in, deposited a breakfast tray on my bedside table, passed in front of me with his ramrod-straight back and opened the heavy velvet curtains. His slim body's lathe-like posture disgusted me; as a child I used to make pacts with the devil to see him crumpled up and sour-faced.

Straightening out my tray, he said, "You cannot know how

worried we were to see you lying in front of the door as though you'd been hit on the head with a sledgehammer," not neglecting to inject a tremor of sorrow in his voice. Impeccable Wang Yu. Who knows to what extent you relished what happened to me?

"Even if it wasn't a sledgehammer, dear Wang Yu," I said, "I would guess that I stopped an empty bottle." If there was one thing Wang Yu couldn't stand it was to be called 'dear Wang Yu' by anyone other than my mother. He was just pacing out of my room when I added: "Ah, dear Wang Yu, I have a request. Would you please go and give my grandfather's office a good clean today? Only, please don't open the windows. You may open the blinds but not the windows on any account."

"Of course," said Wang Yu, "with pleasure." The pleasure he took in saying the phrase 'with pleasure' should have alerted me. Ah, I should have known what was going through that snakish mind of his!

Towards evening, much recovered, I cast aside the ice pack on my head, and throwing my grandfather's trench coat over my back, I headed off for his office. As I entered the building I was horrified: the whole atmosphere of the building had changed. If was as if some mischievous Hindu god had blown all the fresh air of the Himalayas into it. A gentle breeze wafted on every side. The edifice's elderly inhabitants, who had seen better days, ran to and fro from room to room, their cheeks red from an excess of oxygen, their eyes glowing like those of bewitched children. It was impossible not to guess the name of that mischievous god bestowed upon us by the land of India: dear, dear, dear Wang Yu.

Entering the room I was confronted by the surprise that Wang Yu had left: the windows were wide open. The room, madly cleansed to a slippery sheen, seemed to have been turned into one of those immortal pieces of lacquered Chinese art. Holding on left and right, feeling as though I were walking on a waxed tray, I made it to the windows. With all my strength I closed them and made it to the head of the table. My nerves in shreds, my cheeks flushed, from the row of glasses arranged by height on the table, I grabbed the largest one, filled it with whiskey and tilted it back. Just as I was about to relax for a short spell, an elderly gentleman who I assumed to be a neighbour from the third floor came in saying, "Don't get up, please don't get up."

"Goodness gracious," he said, "that man of yours is no servant, he's a ball of fire. He came around to each of us – one by one. If there was a window he opened it. And what a cleaning! He had three helpers at his side. Not just your office, he dusted down the entire building. A blessed ball of fire, I've never seen anything like it. A ball of fire."

"Don't mention it, sir," I said as civilly as possible, "If you have no enemy you have no servant."

Smiling uneasily, he said, "It appears you're staying. It's long past my time to be gone. I thought on my way out I'd drop by. I've never seen anything like it – is he industrious or what? A blessed ball of fire, a ball of fire."

Shaking his hand, I said, "Please do call again, sir. It's been a pleasure meeting you."

"We all loved your grandfather very much," he replied. "We're waiting for you too to drop by one day."

Having bid the gentleman farewell I was seated at my table when, with a terrific force, someone knocked at the door three times at equal intervals. I was no longer in a mood to get up from my seat for unexpected guests. Yesterday one, today two: honestly, the office had become the meeting hall of the building. "The door's open," I called, "please come in."

In came a pale, pretty-faced, soft-brown-haired man in wire-framed glasses. He strode straight for my table carrying a package wrapped in shiny duck-green paper.

He held out his hand and said, "Good evening, I hope I'm not disturbing you. Pardon me for dropping by so unexpectedly. But Monsieur Jacob insisted so strongly that I leave this package with you that I was obliged to disregard the inappropriateness of it all."

His palm was sweaty. While speaking he wasn't looking at my eyes, but at my temples, and every so often he licked his upper lip. He had a pleasant, steady tone of voice and an impeccable manner of speech. But such perfection seemed tedious and even inhuman: coupled with his fine physique, one found oneself calling him 'Robot Man'. If it were up to me to name him, I wouldn't have chosen anything other than Robot Man. As it was, his name had been established long before and it was only left for me to discover it.

"It was very good of you, Mr. Wolfscientist." I said, "There must be a seven-volume horse trainer biography in that package. I'm most pleased. Would you care for a little whiskey?"

"You're right, I am a wolf researcher," he said, smiling. His perfect smile betrayed a certain artificiality. But perhaps everything the man did evoked that sense of unreal perfection. "In short, 'neither a memorable name nor a noteworthy appearance'," he went on mockingly. "I thank you for your offer of whiskey; unfortunately, however, I won't accept it. It affects my gall bladder. Even after a single drop, I'm writhing in such agony, you couldn't imagine. You must be a very dear friend of Monsieur Jacob's. He made such a clamour over it that even though I had only got as far as the third volume, I brought you 'your' biography."

"As you like," I said. "I too have a gift . . . I mean, I too wanted to give you a present. It's waiting for you. Drop by one day."

That was too much! I broke off and fixed my smouldering eyes on his face. I'm not one to speak ineptly or incoherently, but with all his perfection, that man made you speak in such a frothy, absurd way that it got on your nerves. The Irish-Cap-Man came to mind. Perhaps to him we all seem like robots.

For some inexplicable reason my anger and surprise seemed to make Mr. Wolfscientist relax, or at least to open up. "Did you buy something for me?" he asked. "Thank you. Really, thank you so much." He could even laugh with his eyes. Or perhaps this good humour was merely a mask? My suspicious nature evaporates when I drink: it seeks the calf in the cow, the diamond in the hay, the broken-hearted angel in an old robot.

"I wonder if I could help you?" he asked affectionately. "According to Monsieur Jacob, you're dealing with the messenger boy murders."

"Actually, I know so little about the matter of the messenger boys it would be helpful if you could enlighten me on the subject."

"As you may or may not know," he said, clearing his throat, "the messenger boys are one of the wonders of genetic engineering."

"What!" I exclaimed. "Genetic engineering?"

"Without a doubt," he said. "They are all the same; of course, not only in their uniforms, but also in their attitudes and behaviour; in their walk, posture, hair, skin and eye colour, even their dimples. Didn't you ever wonder why they were all so alike?"

"Would you believe," I said, "that until last night, when I dreamt about them, I'd never given any thought to the matter? The messenger boys are just like mailboxes — that is to say, they're so common you don't notice them. Would you ever stop to consider if mailboxes are all alike or not?"

"But they're human," said Mr. Wolfscientist. "And they are being killed one by one." His voice broke: "Last month I was called to examine one of their corpses as there were claw marks on the throat. Oh, to see that lovely, tiny body lying dead by the curb. Believe me, it was unbearable." My throat seemed to tear.

"Yes, very sad. All this is very sad," I said, rather awkwardly. "Please tell me everything you know about them."

"The sperm is taken from the city's most esteemed gentlemen," he said swallowing, his eyes drawn to my replenished glass.

My head hurt like mad, my temples felt as though they were being stabbed, my stomach burned mercilessly. If I drank enough, I could forget all the pain, withdraw from my seized-up body, maintain the desired distance between body and spirit. "Don't pay any attention to me, I insist that you continue," I said. "I only drink at this time of the day."

At last, he looked into my eyes as he spoke. His secretive, slightly slanted, expressionless brown eyes peered out from behind his spectacles. He subdued his feelings and never stammered once.

He continued: "Yes, those most superior gentlemen's most precious sperm is taken and stored, and when the time comes it is injected into messenger boy mothers chosen according to all sorts of genetic criteria. These chosen women are blonde, beautiful, intelligent and very special. They are of course kept under strict control until they give birth. If there is the slightest possibility of deformity they are made to abort – so only the most perfect messenger boys, our city's objects of pride, are allowed to be born. Even with all this precision and calculation, if a baby with light brown hair or one not considered so beautiful was born, every one of the ambition-swollen messenger boy mothers would cry. Wailing that the genes hadn't been properly selected, they would submit to nervous breakdowns. They might even swear never to take part in the project again. These 'flawed' children would immediately be weeded out and put in an orphanage. As it is, this rarely happens. Do you know that in our city there are only seventy to eighty messenger boys? Very little is known about their exact numbers and actual circumstances. They are some sort of enigma."

"I understand, Mr. Wolfscientist," I said (though it was

actually impossible to understand such science fiction). "Do you know how many messenger boys have been killed so far?" I asked, my tongue beginning to lisp. Recently, in my attempts to separate my mind from my body, getting drunk out of my head was becoming a frequent occurrence. But it had nothing to do with what had happened to me recently.

"It's supposed that up until now six, even seven murders have been committed," he said. "I won't say anything definite, for, as you can well imagine, the messenger boys are an extremely sensitive subject. I'm afraid that to the extent you want certainty you'll be in a commensurate amount of trouble. Please — but please — be very careful. Besides, you can call me any time you feel the need for help."

I couldn't help thinking 'compassionate robot angel'! Compassion is one of those concepts I have wracked my brains about but I haven't managed to come to any conclusion. It wasn't difficult to perceive that this serious, unpoetic man was a compassion freak. If there's one thing I know it is that compassion is a great burden for people of poetry. Even if they need it, they can't offer it.

"Believe me, my head is all mixed up," I said. "I guess this is what I deserve, but right now my only wish is to solve this matter. It's so difficult for me . . . " Mr. Wolfscientist-Compassionate-Angel had become quite touched by me, with my blood-shot eyes and my lips sliding left and right.

"Look," he said, "I know you. I know you better than many of those people who think they know you. And believe me, I'm on your side with all my heart. If someone is to solve this, it can only be you. But is it imperative that you solve this; or, is it more important that we oppose the imperatives forced upon us by the objective world? I leave the answer to this entirely up to you."

"There are surprising similarities between scientists and men of religion," I said to Mr. Wolfscientist. "They speak in long and jumbled sentences and they are people without poetry. I don't know if their poetry has been used up or if their heads have become so labyrinthine because they are un-poetic from birth. You are good hearted, sir. Besides, I don't fail to see a playful side in you. Yet how I wish you had even a particle of poetry in you. How I wish! I wish!" He smiled. He smiled a sweet smile. It was a smile that gave me the right to forgive myself.

"It's time for me to go," he said. "There's so much work waiting for me."

"Ah," I said, "I'm very sorry you have to make your living as a stockbroker. That a man as devoted to science as yourself should have to deal with that kind of work every god-given day!"

"Wolves have declined so much," he said. "They're so honourable, they don't compromise. They won't even compromise over the cost of survival. On the other hand, there's the fox! Did you know that in our city tens of thousands of foxes live unbeknownst to us? They only come out at night. From a distance we assume that they're dogs or such, but there they are, in tens of thousands, living right under our noses."

"I have one last question, Mr. Wolfscientist," I said "Did the claw marks found on the messenger boy's throat belong to a wolf?"

"No. You'd be surprised, but they were made by a human hand imitating wolf's claws," he said. "It's impossible to say how it was done but I'm sure the marks were the work of a human hand." He got to his feet, voice shaking. "Wolves are honourable and in any case they are abandoning this world," he said. At that point he quickly pulled himself together and politely bade me farewell.

I realized as he walked straight for the stairs that the back of his head was as flat as a robot's. Behold, I thought, a man who wouldn't love anyone much more than his own honour. He wouldn't fall in love.

As soon as Mr. Wolfscientist left, on a white piece of parchment paper that happened to be resting on the tabletop I wrote:

- *A blow from a human hand impersonating a wolf claw. How and why?*
- *How were the other five or six children murdered?*
- *Who are the messenger boys? Where do they live, how are they raised, how do they die (from natural causes, that is)?*
- *Is there a woman's hand in a red lace glove? Was it that that hit me on the head?*

And lastly:

- *Messenger boy mothers*

I underlined it. Then, stretching out on the table I began to fall asleep. I was in no condition to go home. I didn't have the courage, nor was I in the state to do so.

⚜ ⚜ ⚜ ⚜ ⚜ ⚜

I awoke to my seized-up body, my burning stomach, the sun coming through the windowpanes, the knocking at the door, all assaulting me at once. Rubbing my eyes, I straightened up; I stretched, my arms moved back and forth with difficulty. My head felt like a bag full of pebbles and my mouth was so dry it felt like the inside of a carcass. I lowered the blinds, every bone of my body aching. I was just thinking how my grandfather must have known something for not spending his nights spread out on the table when again there was a knock at the door. It was a determined caller who, with their intermittent pauses, also showed a certain unwillingness.

"Come in," I said in a wretched and hoarse voice. "The door's always open." I filled my glass with whiskey and gulped it down. It seemed to me this was the best way to start the day. My visitor entered and sat in the armchair to my left. "The door's open, always, always open," I said to myself, my voice left over from last night, my head drooping.

"I beg your pardon?" my visitor said.

I looked at her. And looked.

She was blonde and slightly sunburned. Her eyes were the deepest blue, her nose straight and thin, and above her upper lip there was a beauty mark. Her thick blonde hair was tied up, but here and there strands of it dangled free, almost reaching her close-set eyes. She smiled. Only, her smile was absent. Her lips were thin, and her teeth — there was something about her teeth.

"Pardon me," she said again. But her beauty was unforgivable. She lit a cigarette. She began playing with the bandage wound around her hand. She tugged the bandage, pulling a bit of it up as if she were looking at the wound, repeatedly covering it and opening it again. She put out her half-smoked cigarette and focused her close-set blue eyes on mine. "My name's Esme," she said. "I'm a messenger boy mother."

I had no choice but to refill my glass (Oh, tell me reader, did I have any other choice?).

"Monsieur Jacob sent me," she said. "He guessed that you wouldn't go home but would pass out in your office. He definitely wanted me to come, so here I am. I must have woken you up. But the sunshine was peeking through your door, and anyway, it's twelve o'clock. Besides, I don't think you should stay hunched over your table."

She spoke very slowly, elongating her words. She had a strange voice, a broken accent. She spoke as if she'd been raised on some continent on the farthest side of the ocean and later returned to our city. I really had to struggle to follow what she was saying.

She took out from her bag a huge bar of chocolate with pistachio nuts. "Could I have a glass of whiskey?" she asked. "Though not as much as you. I too have a certain fondness for the stuff. I hope that you won't say no to some chocolate."

"One couldn't say I have an addictive personality," I said. "But chocolate, especially chocolate with pistachios, is something I am quite fond of."

I took one of the clean glasses from my table, filled it with whiskey and passed it to her. She polished it off, and with that strange voice from the farthest shore of the ocean she said: "My nerves are shot. The other day I burned my hand fixing the fuse. I burned myself to the bone. Every now and then, my mind is somewhere else. I either cut my hands or I burn them. I have a pair of — how do you say it? — accident-prone hands. Probably I just don't know where to put them."

"You don't look like someone who would put them in a pair of red lace gloves," I said. I broke off a piece of chocolate and tossed it in my mouth.

Her unbandaged hand dived into her huge and chaotic bag and came out with a pair of red lace gloves. "We all have a pair," she said. "That is, all the messenger boy mothers. Why red, I don't know. I hate red. Anyway, it gets on my nerves — we're obliged to wear these when we visit them. They loathe any kind of physical contact. We're mothers, too, no matter how weird a way we became so. We want to touch them; sometimes we can't control ourselves. They feel more comfortable because we have these lace gloves on our hands. We have the right to visit them three times a week. At three hours a visit that makes nine hours in total. Those nine hours really do you in; for the rest of the week you're in no condition to do anything else. Aside from cutting and burning your hands, of course."

Esme became teary-eyed. To see her like that was unbearable.

I wanted to leave on the first ship from port; I also wanted to stay nailed to that table. I endured what seemed like several centuries while she sat across the table and spoke. Esme really was very beautiful. She was very beautiful and very special.

"Last night my son was killed," she said. "Or at least, last night another messenger boy was murdered and I think he was one of the ones I gave birth to. I'm the mother of two messenger boys. They don't really want us to know which messenger boys are ours. They encourage some kind of collective motherhood. But by the birth date, intuition, this and that, we can figure out who our children are and of course we behave somewhat differently with them. That boy, he was my little son and very sweet; so very, very sweet. Maybe I'm just being silly, but he seemed to me to be more sensitive, more thoughtful than the others. Look, messenger boys are so perfect, so — how shall I say it? — frightful, you wouldn't believe it. Because of their fathers, because of the way they're brought up . . . Always scientists, philosophers, men of religion — for this business they always use the sperm of men who exist through their brains. All of them are like robots. It's absolutely forbidden for the mothers to know from which person the sperm was taken. But I got into the files at the hospital. The father of my dead son is a famous wolf scientist but he makes his living as a stockbroker. He's such a soulless, uninspiring person. If you saw him the first thing that you would think is that he's a robot."

I again emptied my newly-filled glass in one tilt. I started eating the chocolate with relish. There definitely is a connection between eating chocolate and unhappiness — definitely.

"Esme," I said, "please tell me everything I need to know. How these children grow up, where they grow up, how many children there are, why they are — yes it's patently obvious they are very useful to our city — but whose idea were these children anyway and why are they being killed one by one?"

"There are exactly thirty-three messenger boys," she said. "Including my son last night, seven messenger boys have been murdered. So that's how many are left out of forty. Everyone thinks that because they all look alike and can be anywhere at any time that there are many more of them. There are those who assume that there are seventy, eighty — even as many as a hundred. From thirteen messenger boy mothers," she gulped, "forty messenger boys." She stopped. "I'm a deviant messenger boy mother," she said. "I'm not cut out for this work. When I returned to this city I wanted to be a mother. I took several tests of course: intelligence exams, character tests, health tests, genetic tests. I was extremely qualified, very eligible. Now they regret a thousand times over having chosen me. As for giving birth to those two children — no, I don't regret that. I couldn't have been a mother any other way. I'm both a mother and I'm not. Anyway, that's the only way I could do it."

"But why messenger boy motherhood?" I asked. "You could have been a mother by normal means." By letting this question leave my lips, I seemed the rudest and most unimaginative person on earth. My face went crimson.

"You'd want to have a child from a man with whom you'd had good memories," she said. "Good memories are accumulated with daily life. I can't bear the tedium of daily life. I can only endure loneliness. It seemed a good idea to become a messenger boy mother. Please understand."

She began unwrapping her bandage furiously. The wound was broad and deep, and it hadn't fully closed.

"Esme," I said, "could I insist that you wrap up that bandage? I can't stand seeing wounds. I can't stand seeing wounds, accidents, or corpses. Seven messenger boys have been murdered one by one. One of them was found with claw marks on his throat but how he was killed isn't known. Who knows how last night's was killed — or the ones before for that matter? Do I have to think

about these things? What are these murders to me? Every one of
these boys is an angelic copy made by artificial insemination;
intelligent, well mannered and flawless. There's a good reason
for every murder, just as for suicide. People lead such meaningless, boring lives in this city. Nobody is interested in having me
'solve' these 'normal' lives. They don't demand that I investigate
how they manage to bear such miserable, tedious lives. But then
there are seven murders, and lo and behold, I'm charged with
finding the reason behind the messenger boy murders. I sometimes even find it hard to tie my own shoelaces. And now I'm
expected to put an end what may be one of the most wonderful
things ever to have occurred in this city. As for you, please, don't
open your bandage again."

Esme's close-set eyes opened wide. "I'm sorry," she said. "I like
looking at my wounds, but if it makes you uncomfortable . . .
Look how nicely I wrapped it, but not again — I won't open it
again until after I leave your office."

She smiled sweetly and I couldn't help smiling, too — it was
impossible not to.

"Look, now I'll answer your questions," she said. "Maybe it
will help you. So, hmmm, what were they? What did you ask me?"

"Where are they raised?" I said.

"In messenger boy houses," she said. "Until they are two
they're raised in a laboratory-like place. Later they are taken
from there and brought to the homes. If I'm not mistaken
there are five or six. They're all adjacent to each other and they
share the same courtyard. Until the age of two they are raised
in the laboratory like some rare flower, like a brain in a jar —
anyway, something like that — they're raised in isolation. Later
on, in their own homes, they take over their own upbringing.
The older ones show the little ones how to be precise and so
on — they teach them all the finer points of the art of being
messenger boys.

Here they start meeting with the mothers, if you can call that meeting. Don't think that they are in closer contact with us than they are with the rest of you. All us mothers are obliged to come and to leave at the same times. We can never know their secret world. It's impossible for us to teach them anything. By the time they're two they've learned to read and write — forget reading and writing, they've learned everything in the so-called classical education that we toiled in our teens and twenties to learn. Since they learn their way of life from the other messenger boys, and as they're estranged from, and almost disgusted by us, we're merely a bother to them that they have to endure. They're so cold, so distant, that . . . believe me, you can sometimes feel like strangling them."

After saying this, she stopped and burst into laughter. "The murderer is the mother," she said. "Anyway, I didn't kill my son. Or the others. I don't think you'd have wanted to deal with the murders if they were that easy to solve. There's also a good side to those curious creatures," she said, smiling widely again. "It's true; they do have a hidden side. Sometimes a hint of this trickles out. You can't help thinking that these beings are so different, so sensitive that they can't help but hide themselves. You don't have a clue about what they read, what they listen to, what they do in those horrible hospital- or prison-like homes. Ah, but I do know this: they wash all the time; they starch, iron, and wash clothes; they smell of soap from head to toe — and they listen to Mahler. One day, out of stubbornness and curiosity, I arrived at the meeting place early. The guard at the courtyard entrance had fallen asleep. I could hear Mahler playing from one of the houses. Later on, someone saw me, and shhhhhhh: silence again. Silence . . . "

Esme stopped and lit her fifteenth cigarette. I didn't know the exact figure but the ashtray was full of butts. She'd light a cigarette, take two or three puffs, forget it in the ashtray, light another again and put it out half-smoked. When she wasn't fiddling with the cigarettes she brushed at her hair with her hand, pushing it back, then brushing it away again when it fell. Her hands didn't stay still for a moment.

"I want to give you something that will bring you luck," I said to Esme. In fact it was abundantly clear that what she needed was peace of mind, not luck. But pinning names on other peoples' needs always sounds wrong to me. I got up and walked straight to the coat rack. I removed the key-ring from the pocket of my grandfather's trench coat and separated it from the keys. As I passed by her, I placed it in front of her. She immediately picked it up.

"Woooww," she said with that voice from the farthest shore of the ocean. "The eyes of Murugan, the eyes of Murugan, the eyes . . . " I was astonished: it would have been more likely for me to fall from a cherry tree and break my neck than for Esme to know of Murugan.

"I was born in India and lived there till the age of seven," she explained. "I even did my doctorate on the Hindu Pantheon. Here, use this as your key-chain." From amidst her hair she pulled out a huge earring and handed it over. It was a very beautiful silver Pegasus.

"Your office is stuffed full of old movie magazines," she said. "But this one here, this, the one with Humphrey Bogart on the cover — would you give it to me? For me, there's the whole world, and then there's Humphrey Bogart."

"With pleasure," I said. "Besides, there's someone I've met recently. If you take that magazine, you'll save him from going crazy. He's in love with Lauren Bacall and he's quite upset that he doesn't resemble Bogart. At our first and last meeting we polished off a bottle together."

Esme shook with laughter. The whiskey had done the trick: we were both quite drunk.

She stopped laughing suddenly and announced: "I've got to go. It's my son's — or rather, I'm not sure if he's my son or not — but anyway, some messenger boy's funeral. All the mothers — with our tears, our perfect postures, and our black outfits — we have to be ready and in attendance at the ceremony. Messenger boy bodies are burned in a special oven. It could happen, you know — someone might dare to dissect and analyze, to cut one up to discover something about these perfect creatures." She seemed to laugh, but then broke into sobs. "Believe me, he was sweeter, more sensitive than the others."

"Once, he gave me a flower that he'd secretly picked from their garden. Of course I didn't save it. I throw everything away. I don't hold onto memories and such. I wish I had pressed and dried it in a book, I wish . . . "

She lit a last cigarette. "Oh, anyway," she said. "Even if I had saved it I would have burned it today. I can't stand collecting memories."

She got up and when she reached the door she turned to me and said, "Take care of yourself. Thanks for Murugan and Bogart — in a way, they're both the same person."

She pulled the door behind her. I thought that I should be going home, too. I should go home and take a bath.

﹉ ﹉ ﹉ ﹉ ﹉ ﹉

Waiting for me at home was some fish soup, potato salad, a quince dessert, and some good news: my mother had gone to the summer house.

"We were very concerned when you didn't come home yesterday," said Wang Yu, "verrry." Wang Yu's 'royal we' referred to himself and my mother.

"Your esteemed mother wore herself out with worry saying, 'Ah, where could that child be?' She gave me specific instructions:

'Do save the fish soup for the child, Wang Yu,' she said. And to her I said: 'Of course, my lady. Of course I know that you cooked that fish soup for the little one!'"

"Yes, Wang Yu," I said. "No one is better at receiving and carrying out instructions than you. Tell me, did my grandfather go to a lot of trouble to find you? I'm sure there was no one else like you in the whole state of Maharashtra."

"Wang Yu doesn't enjoy discussing this subject," Wang Yu replied. So he closed the subject by turning his back on me and launching into his endless kitchen chores.

Why did my grandfather bring Wang Yu back from Bombay? Why the name Wang Yu? To what could one attribute his reticence, his sulkiness whenever he was the subject of discussion?

Let life flow; let it pass in front of you like a trickling stream. Once you start tampering with it, there is no end. You'll only be submerged by all that water. You'll either drown or end up opening your eyes to the open sea – and then there's no turning back.

"Wang Yu," I said. "I'm very tired. I want to take a bath and go to bed. If possible, don't wake me for anything. I want to sleep undisturbed until the morning."

"Of course," said Wang Yu. "Whatever you wish."

But by now, you can imagine what my fate would be: it was my karma to be woken by a knock at the door. I had been asleep for only one or two hours when Wang Yu knocked at the door and said, "I beg your pardon." He opened the door gently and continued: "There is a messenger boy waiting downstairs for you. No matter what I said, I couldn't send him away. It seems he has a message that he simply must deliver to you."

"Alright, Wang Yu," I said. "Invite him to the sitting room. I'll get dressed and come down immediately."

As I went down the stairs, I saw his slim, elegant body seated on the edge of one of the beige armchairs. He was distracted; his eyes seemed far away and full of pain. I moved very quietly.

He hadn't even noticed that I'd come in. I thought to myself, "what a tiny body, what a perfect face." It's impossible to discern the age of messenger boys. Whether six or twenty-six, they always look the same age. They are the miraculous children of genetic engineering: they don't grow up, they don't get wrinkled, they don't shrivel. Somehow, I felt that the one waiting for me there was one of the older ones. Who knows, perhaps he was about to hit thirty — the oldest among them. Eight or ten years ago the newspapers had trumpeted some news about the messenger boys: two twenty-year-old messenger boys had developed a heart condition, one after the other. Their deaths were featured everywhere. It was speculated that their demise was due to the injections that stopped them from growing and kept them looking like children. The question was raised as to why they existed in the first place and then, as always, the topic subsided from public scrutiny. From all this, though, one thing was determined: messenger boys live to the age of thirty, thirty-five at most. Now, the oldest of them had to be nearing thirty. And maybe the one sitting there in the armchair, giving away his age with his eyes, was precisely that one. I quivered with excitement.

"Good evening, messenger boy," I said. "It seems there is some news you wanted to give me."

Before saying yes, he pulled himself together. Into those clear blue eyes he inserted that vacant, placid expression — he slipped into the messenger boy countenance.

"Monsieur Jacob wanted me to deliver this note to you; presumably, it is very important. Your servant said you were sleeping. I was obliged, however, to insist. I hope you will forgive me."

"Not to worry. You're most welcome, messenger boy," I said. "In fact it's very good you came; I wanted to ask you a few questions about messenger boys."

"In the City Library — under the letter M," he said. "If you wish I can give you directions to the library. As for the alphabet, I imagine you know it. If you look under the heading 'Messenger Boy' you can learn everything about us that you may wish to know — maybe even more."

His voice was like ice. I was taken aback; I was stunned by what I had come up against. This must have been what Esme was talking about. In the company of these monuments to wisdom, you could be done for in a minute.

"Good evening," he said.

"Good evening, messenger boy," I replied.

There wasn't a soul in the city who didn't know I was dealing with the messenger boy murders. So, was this peevish manner, this state of loathing, their standard reaction to anyone who stuck their nose into their affairs? My thoughts got stuck on the word loathing: Esme had used that word. I opened and read the note the messenger boy had brought.

It was a note written in green ink by Monsieur Jacob's shaky, age-blotched hand.

> *Beloved friend,*

it began.

> *I've learned something concerning the messenger boy who was murdered last night . . . Come to my shop at once. In any case, there is a great deal more we have to talk about. I'll tell you everything that you wanted to know! Pay attention to the messenger boy who brought you this note. Ask him one or two questions if you wish. Where is the City Library? I can tell you how to get there. The letter M comes after the letter L and before the letter N. Ha, ha, ha! Joking aside, get here before I close my shop.*
>
> *Yours always,*

It was signed:

Jacob

I seemed to be going mad. It was as if I was a puppet in Jacob's play. He sent all those people banging on my door; he knew what had happened and what was going to happen to me; even worse, he diagnosed the things swirling around in my head and provided answers for them. Now, if I was dealing with these ridiculous murders instead of sitting down and reading my horse trainer biography, it was all because of Jacob! With these thoughts churning around in my head I careened madly through the streets until I arrived at the duck-green wooden door of Jacob's shop.

"My goodness, dear friend, my goodness, my goodness!" he greeted me so heartily one might have thought I'd returned from a seven-year voyage.

"Monsieur Jacob," I said sulkily, "did you specially choose that cute messenger boy or are all the little darlings so affable?"

"Up until now have you thought about it at all?" asked Jacob. "Have you thought at all about what they are like, where they live, how they're raised, how they die? Messenger boy here, messenger boy there. We all know that they are clever, refined, flawless. That they can be anywhere at any time. They are an extraordinary luxury provided by our wealthy city. But they are not machines, my dear. Despite everything, they're human beings."

"I don't know, Monsieur Jacob," I said. "At this point I don't know what to think. It's obvious that they are very useful to us. They are also a symbol of our wealth, our advancement, our ability to kneed genes any way we want. But still, why were these children created? Isn't it a very treacherous guinea pig project?"

"Who knows," said Jacob. "Maybe they ask this very same question themselves. Listen, don't look at these events so simplistically. Think of a tall building. You're still wandering around on the building's lowest floor. When you get out onto the roof and look around, you'll see everything – the City Council, the mothers, the messenger boys. Only then will you see everything."

"Ah, something came to mind when you mentioned mothers," I said. "Actually, it never leaves my mind. Thank you for sending Esme to me. It was very beneficial to talk with her. And what's more, she's the most beautiful woman I've ever seen."

"Esme?" he said. "Who's Esme?"

"Come on, she's that messenger boy mother." I said. "You sent her to see me only this morning. A blonde, very beautiful woman."

"All messenger boy mothers are blonde and 'very' beautiful," said Jacob in a cross manner. "I didn't send any Esme to you. There was a ridiculous man who showed up at my shop. He really insisted on meeting you. I sent him to you, along with that other one – what was his name? – the one who bought your biography. The one you made such a story about. The Wolfscientist – I sent him."

"Monsieur Jacob," I said, "what are you saying? You didn't send Esme to me?"

"Noooo, my good friend," he said bursting into laughter. "She told you a bold-faced lie."

Suddenly I was assaulted by those red lace gloves, what Esme had said, and my dream. Why do we believe women so easily? Just because they're more open, more vulnerable; because they seem pleasant and warm; because they gain our affection and can see into our hearts? Esme had deceived me.

"Forget about it, my dear," said Jacob. "You'll solve this mystery. So now listen to what I have to say. Figure this one out: how was last night's messenger boy killed? Clue: Hamlet."

"Please, Monsieur Jacob," I said. "First that messenger boy upset me, then Esme. How would I know how he was killed? Or could it be that poison was poured into his ear like

Hamlet's father?"

"Yes, exactly!" said Jacob clapping his hands. "It happened exactly like that. Now whether you wanted to or not, you'd have to assume this: the murderer in question is well educated. Moreover, a literary type. As for the wolf claw marks on the neck of the previous boy . . . well, what do you say to that?"

"I was going to say Little Red Riding Hood – what should I say?" I responded curtly. "Alright, what about Julius Caesar? Weren't there any victims stabbed in the back?"

"There were," said Jacob, his eyes shining. "There were, my friend. One was found with knife wounds all down the back, from head to toe. But this last one, it really was incredible. *Hamlet* is one of my favourite plays. I believe *Hamlet* is a classic play about youth. With his hatred for everyone and everything, his suspicion, his enmity, Hamlet is a true young man. He loathes everyone around him, starting with Ophelia. In his eyes, everyone is weak, lacking, unreliable. Those magnificent rages; those mad interrogations of himself and his dreams! Ah, how he insults his mother, Polonius, Ophelia! Layer upon layer of insults – two or three meanings in each one!"

"Monsieur Jacob," I said with impatience, "if you have nothing further to tell me, then with your permission . . . I have work to do."

"I've said what I had to, in fact even more," said the old goat, rocking with laughter. He was enjoying himself. A literary murder suspect – one fond of *Hamlet* no less – had made Jacob's day.

Suddenly, he stopped laughing and said, "You mustn't be prejudiced towards the messenger boys. Every one of them is a good and worthy human being."

Monsieur Jacob spoke of them as "human". Mr. Wolfscientist had also referred to them as "human". But what was the truth; who were they?

"Good evening, Monsieur Jacob," I said. "You've shed new light on *Hamlet* — and on the perpetrator of the murders, of course."

"Good evening," he said. "And for goodness sake, wrap your scarf well round your neck. It's become quite chilly."

As soon as I got home I sat down in one of the chairs at the round mahogany table in the middle of my room, and on a piece of white parchment paper that just happened to be at hand, I wrote:

> *Esteemed Mr. Wolfscientist,*
>
> *I was extremely surprised to learn that a test tube containing the precious sperm extracted from the most esteemed gentlemen of this city was indeed yours. How you could participate as a procreator in such an inhuman project is totally inexplicable. It is apparent that you must have given up on resisting the conditions imposed on us by this "objective" world long ago.*
>
> *In the hope that it will be of benefit to you in your work, I'm sending you the book entitled*
>
> *WOLVES: CHANGING MATING PATTERNS UNDER ECOLOGICAL PRESSURE*
>
> *which fell on my head in Monsieur Jacob's shop on the first day I became involved in this case. As to this interest of yours, and as to your own radically changed mating patterns, I leave the judgement entirely up to you.*
>
> *Respectfully yours,*

I signed the note and put it in an envelope. I summoned Wang Yu. "Call one of those twenty-four hour courier centres," I said.

"Alright," he said. He turned his ramrod-straight back on me and went out.

Ten minutes later, Wang Yu ushered a messenger boy into my room.

"Good evening, messenger boy," I said.

"Good evening," he replied.

All messenger boys have the same tone of voice and manner of speaking, yet this messenger boy seemed to have a different, chirpy quality to his voice. "This one is very young," I thought to myself, perhaps only six or seven years old. Either my intuition about messenger boys was developing due to my recent excessive interest in them, or I was completely deluding myself.

"Dear messenger boy," I said, surprising myself over how I'd come up with that "dear" word. "You'll take that book with this letter to our city's renowned wolf researcher. I don't know his real name but he is often referred to as Mr. Wolfscientist. Apparently, in order to make a living he now works as a stockbroker."

"Of course," said the messenger boy.

"Also, I'd like to send a spoken message to someone. Her name is Esme — I don't know, maybe you've met?"

"Yes," said the messenger boy. "She is one of the messenger boy mothers."

"One of your mothers, that is," I said, not able to restrain myself.

"We have exactly thirty-four mothers," he said. "We live in nine houses grouped round a courtyard. Esme visits house numbers three and four far more often then she visits the one where I live. For that reason I can only say that I know her from a distance."

"Thirty-four mothers!" I exclaimed. "So now if you don't object, could I learn how many messenger boys there are in our city?'

"Of course," he said. "All this is recorded under the letter M in the City Library. Nicholai — the other messenger boy who called by earlier today — told you all this. In total we are seventy messenger boys. As you also know, up until today, seven messenger boys have been murdered. So we are what's left from a total of seventy-seven messenger boys."

"Seventy messenger boys," I inquired insistently, "thirty-four mothers?"

"Yes, except that three of them later gave up being messenger boy mothers and became mothers by normal means. Now they're busy raising their own children in their happy homes. For this reason the exact number of mothers who work professionally as messenger boy mothers is thirty-one. In the City Library – "

"Yes, messenger boy," I said. "I'm sure all this is can be found under the letter M in the City Library."

So she'd lied to me. About the numbers, about Jacob. And I'd swallowed the whole story; I'd been fooled.

"Would you go immediately to Esme's and tell her to come to my office tomorrow?" I said, my voice tinged with rage. "Before you even deliver the book with the letter to Mr. Wolfscientist."

"Of course," he said. Did his eyes sparkle with mischief, or was I imagining it?

"Also, even if it's all recorded at the City Library, I'd like to ask how old the eldest of you is?"

"The eldest recently turned thirty," he said. "Nine years ago, the two oldest messenger boys among us developed a heart condition at the age of twenty-two and died. As of yet, except for them, there have been no other deaths from natural causes. I believe this was going to be your next question."

"Yes, messenger boy," I said. "It was. So, the one who came to me earlier today with the message from Monsieur Jacob, is he the eldest?"

He paused and swallowed. "Yes," he blurted. "He is the eldest of us."

"Thank you, dear messenger boy," I said. "Thank you very much for all this information."

"Good evening," he said.

"Good evening," I replied.

He headed straight for the door, but just as he was about to go out, I called, "Messenger boy! Messenger boy, there's a blot of mud on the back of your sock."

He turned and looked at the back of his sock. With a distant, indifferent expression he said, "Really, is that so?" He closed the door softly and was gone.

A thoroughly different sort of messenger boy, I thought. He had even allowed mud to splash on the back of his pompommed stockings. This was completely beyond belief. What about Esme's lies: weren't they also beyond belief?

∗ ∗ ∗ ∗ ∗ ∗

The next morning I got up early and had a good breakfast. I was absolutely determined to abstain from drink the whole day, to see only briefly whoever dropped by, and to concentrate on getting to the bottom of all the convoluted stories I'd heard. I walked boldly through the city's winding streets and arrived at the office. My glass, and Esme's, still stood on the oak table. I took her glass in hand and looked at it: the lipstick traces left by her fine lips rekindled my wrath. She'd out and out lied to me — but why?

"I don't think you'd have wanted to deal with the murders if they were that easy to solve." Her laughter echoed in my ears. Returning from the farthest shore of the ocean back to our city. Her childhood spent in India. Her messenger boy motherhood venture. A doctorate on the Hindu Pantheon. That severe burn on her hand. Her close-set eyes. The pistachio nut chocolate . . . It seemed like a good idea to try to calm down a bit. I filled up my glass and tilted it back.

After filling my third glass, I threw the empty bottle in the bin. That was the last remaining bottle of my grandfather's whiskey. I believe the hours had crept into the afternoon. Without whiskey or books, behind drawn blinds, what could I do in that office that had begun to submerge me in gloom? Esme hadn't come and wasn't going to. She was one of those women who don't show up at the time and place they are expected. She was one of those women who showed up impulsively while you, with your swollen heart, had given up waiting. She was one of those whose unreliability set your nerves on edge. Esme was one of those forgetful ones. What a mighty fortress forgetfulness is; what a formidable coat of armour! Sitting there full of fury and envy I once more hated those who are capable of forgetting; those who can forget, and those who are late.

I was struck with relief when there was a loud bang at the door. In any event, it was far more pleasant and comforting to spend the evening with the Irish-Cap-Man than to sit here alone, eating my heart out. "Open up, please open up!" he shouted, violently pounding on the door. To quiet down his yelling I shouted, "The door's open. It's always open!"

He came tumbling in. Holding proudly a bottle of Johnny Walker Black Label, he resembled a hunter returning victoriously from the chase with his prey in hand.

"Yes, my good man," I said. "You've hit the nail on the head. Like anyone who knows what's what, Johnny Walker Black Label is my first choice and this glass you see in my hand has just dispatched with the last of the whiskey in this room. Thank you — well done!"

Among the curious properties of drink is its propensity to cause one to be amazingly vulgar. Upon reading my response to the Irish-Cap-Man, I suspect that you, too, are of the same opinion.

I filled my self-draining glass and his blue one to the brim, and we drank together. From the inside pocket of his jacket, he produced an ID photo and placed it in front of me. It was of Lauren Bacall. One would have to imagine that finding a picture belonging to Lauren Bacall, especially an ID photo, was no easy task.

"Amazing," I said. "There's nothing you wouldn't do for her. Wasn't it difficult to find her ID shot?"

"When it comes to her," he said with his eyelids fluttering, "my ties to daily life are cut. Severed — just like that. I no longer think about mundane things, see the difference between easy or hard, long or short — it doesn't matter. That's what love is all about! You cut yourself off from this b-b-b- boring life, and you run!"

"I met a woman infatuated with Humphrey Bogart," I said. "And what's more, she's a true liar."

"Oh, for goodness sake!" he shouted, shaking with laughter. It could only happen to y-y-you, y-you! Women infatuated with Bogart — stay away from such women!" He was laughing and shaking so much that he only just managed to finish his words and it seemed he might fall out of his armchair.

"There's no responding to your joy," I said, feeling that his mirth was no longer bearable.

But suddenly he stopped. "Women who love Bogart are unreliable women," he said. "This has been scientifically proven."

"How?" I queried. "Scientifically how?"

"That is, I-I-I- think so," he said and then he laughed so hard that he sprayed spittle over half the table.

This dottiness had gone too far. I was no longer in the mood to put up with him. I replenished my glass. At that moment, there were three striking knocks at the door: knocks neither long nor short but with equal pauses between them.

"The door is always open, Mr. Wolfscientist," I responded.

He came in. After greeting us politely with a nod, he sat down in the armchair across from the Irish-Cap-Man. His thick brown hair, cut in tiers, was quite long: it came down to his eyebrows.

In this state, his head resembled a giant artichoke. I thought to myself that he needed a good barber — wouldn't it be better if that beautiful face were more visible?

He rested on his knees his clearly very expensive leather bag and began to fiddle with its handle. As he flipped the handle back and forth, he would every so often lick his upper lip.

Avoiding contact with my eyes and looking at my temples, he began to speak in his unfaltering voice and perfect diction.

"I received the book and the letter that you sent me last night, thank you. So first I want to thank you, and then I'd like to warn you in a friendly manner. I would like to seriously caution you against assuming such an accusatory tone and coming to conclusions without first understanding all the dimensions."

At the end of this pompous delivery, the Irish-Cap-Man burst into laughter. He laughed in such a way, gripping his belly and lunging backwards and forwards, that I too started laughing. Mr. Wolfscientist's composure was undisturbed. He gently wiped with his hand the spittle that the Irish-Cap-Man had sprayed on his face and fixed his cold eyes on mine.

"B-b-believe me, I-I-I'm listening to you," I said, half-managing to suppress my laughter.

"Above anything else, the messenger boys are an industry," he said. "Messenger boy motherhood isn't only one of the most prestigious occupations in this city, it is also one of the most highly paid. When it comes to messenger boy fatherhood — " he paused, swallowed, and cleared his throat. "There is no institution of fatherhood as such; there's only the commercial fact of selling the sperm. The amount paid for the sperm is very high, and seven years ago, I had no choice but to get involved in this business. I have no need to tell you whether or not I regret what I did, but if one were to question the institution of the messenger boys then yes, I'm against it. And today, if I were to mobilize all of my material and moral resources in opposing not only this, but all decisions taken by the City Council that I disagree with politically . . . "

At that point, such a bold burst of laughter erupted from the Irish-Cap-Man's mouth (who since last I spoke had been clamping it shut with his hand), that Mr. Wolfscientist had to cut his speech. Without looking me in the face, he rose and shook my hand in farewell. The palms of his hands were sweaty and his gait was anxious and hurried. Thrusting each foot forward, he almost ran out of the room. Perhaps he would have been better off giving a bit of the care he lavished on his speech to his walk. And he definitely needed a haircut.

Between fits of laughter, the Irish-Cap-Man, again spraying forth his spittle, began shouting: "He's a robot! A robot!" Unfortunately, as he shut the door, Mr. Wolfscientist overheard these words. I wondered what I should do – especially as I agreed with the Irish-Cap-Man that Mr. Wolfscientist was indeed practically a robot.

After the Irish-Cap-Man got over his laughing fit, he fixed his calm and innocent eyes on mine. They reminded me of a dog's. Then he asked, "Please tell me, do you like the Rolling Stones?"

"Yes, my good man," I said. "Like anyone who knows what's what, the Rolling Stones are my favourite. I can imagine they are very important to you. Forgive me, but I might even go so far as to say that you have an addictive personality."

"Say it then," he responded, suddenly sad. "Yes, ye-ye-yes you're right: I have an addictive personality. Look, I've had a line from one of my favourite songs tattooed on my arm." He had recovered his old joy. "I had it done in another city while on a business trip," he said, now having a hard time restraining his laughter.

I couldn't help but wonder who would employ a man like him.

Probably he had inherited a snail factory or some such business from his father.

"Now," he said mischievously, "guess which line I chose for my arm."

"It must be 'I can't get no satisfaction'," I replied vacantly.

"Oh-hoh!" he shouted. "No, you didn't get it, you didn't get it! It was 'Don't play with me 'cause you play with fire'."

"Hmm, that's not bad," I replied to my compulsory guest. He was silly, but at least he was entertaining. Yet, I was bored with him, especially as my mind was wandering elsewhere. "Don't you have to pick up your mother this evening and take her home, or don't you have somewhere else to go . . . anything to do? The first time you came by you got really anxious," I said.

Suddenly he looked at his watch: "It's seven o'clock!" he exclaimed. "You're so intelligent, you're really a lifesaver. You'ı r-r-right, I was supposed to pick my mother up at six to take hɛ to the doctor. A tyrannical woman! I'm r-r-ruined," he sai catapulting from his seat.

He stuffed his overcoat under his arm and grabbed his cap. "Goodbye," he shouted. He made such a clamour as he descended the stairway that my desk shook.

"Don't play with me 'cause you play with fire." I laughed to myself. What a silly man! And, Esme hadn't shown up. Nor would she later. I got up from my spot and took my grandfather's trench coat. I dug my hand in the pocket, took out the silver Pegasus and looked at it. It was beautiful and special. She was a bit of a liar, a bit crazy, and a bit drunk. There was no need to get hung up on it, none at all.

After the Irish-Cap-Man left, I had no desire to remain in the office. But who should I encounter wandering home through the city's winding streets? Wang Yu, drunk as a skunk! The Indians have a drink called *arrack*, a few shots of which make it hard for you to remain on your feet.

"For goodness sake, Wang Yu," I said, "I would have sooner imagined that I'd fall from a plum tree and break my neck than see you drunk like this."

"Our crow came to mind," he said.

"Your crow?" I responded. "Of course, when you drink, your crow comes to mind! What crow, whose crow?"

"The Madagascan crow," he said.

"Ahh, is that so?" I said.

"Wang Yu loved your grandfather very much," he continued. "Wang Yu would have given his life for your grandfather. Our crow was very clever; he recited Shakespeare sonnets that your grandfather taught him."

One can be confronted by many unbearable things in life, yet surely a Madagascan crow that recites Shakespeare's sonnets tops the list.

"Your grandfather loved Shakespeare very much," he said. "Even before teaching me to read or write your grandfather made me memorize Hamlet's tirades."

"*Hamlet* is a play about youth," I said, "a classic play of youth." By discussing Shakespeare, even for an instant I, too, could feel like a Madagascan crow.

"How did it go?" wondered Wang Yu in a cracked, high-pitched voice. "Yes, yes, it went like this:

> *Shall I compare thee to a summer's day?*
> *Thou art more lovely and temperate.*
> *Rough winds do shake the darling buds of May,*
> *And summer's lease hath all too short a date.*

Our crow recited that quatrain without a stutter. That was the first quatrain of your grandfather's favourite sonnet. Mine too, of course. Everything that he loved, I loved too."

Ah, an Indian servant who can recite sonnets from Shakespeare is without a doubt every bit as surprising as a Madagascan crow.

And, oh observant reader, didn't the same thought cross your mind that crossed mine: Is the servant the murderer?

That night, I could have made Wang Yu talk a long, long time. I could have learned anything I wanted to. One couldn't say I have a principled character; but to peel back the skin of an inebriated person and look inside is something I would never wish to attempt.

"Just go to bed, Wang Yu," I said, "and don't upset yourself. There's just one thing I'd like to ask you: What was the name of your crow?"

"It was Angela," he said. "We just called her Angela. She also liked her name very much."

I didn't ask him why his name was Wang Yu. I just said, "Goodnight, Wang Yu."

And he said goodnight too.

That night I was proud of myself for having behaved in such a thoughtful and noble manner.

⬥ ⬥ ⬥ ⬥ ⬥ ⬥

In spite of, or more likely because of the fact that I was unspeakably tired, I didn't sleep until late. And even though I dearly wanted to, I didn't start reading my horse trainer biography either. I clasp onto a book from the beginning, cutting myself off from all connections with the world and allowing myself to live only in the midst of those pages. Since my childhood I have never compromised on my loyalty to books. And since it would take me days to complete the seven volumes, and as I had a burning need to air my head a bit, I read, as I usually do at such times, tales from Hans Christian Andersen.

The first light of day was licking the heavy velvet curtains of my room when I turned off the marble lamp on my bedside table. As so often happens in my sleep, I remember twice falling into a deep abyss and violently landing on my bed.

In my dream a messenger boy was breathlessly running through the city's deserted streets shouting, "Mother! Mother!" He wasn't just any messenger boy. He was the young messenger boy I'd sent to Esme and Mr. Wolfscientist, the one with mud splattered on the back of his sock. He ran, terrified, through the city, and in the distance a Madagascan crow with its cracked voice sang the tune, *A Rabbit Was Sleeping in the Ditch*. Suddenly, from out of the gloom, a gigantic man in black appeared at a street corner. He was wearing a pair of silver cowboy boots with pointed toes and high, pointed brown heels. He was furiously stamping into the ground a pair of red lace gloves, from which came the sound of sobs. Meanwhile the messenger boy turned into a cul-de-sac. The silver-booted man went on crushing the gloves as the gloves cried buckets. The messenger boy's pom-pommed socks were smeared with blood as he stood breathlessly in that dead-end street calling out, "Mother! Mother! Mother!"

I woke up in a sweat. Had something happened to that sweet, lovely messenger boy? Hating myself for having fallen asleep in my bed reading Hans Christian Andersen's *Fairy Tales*, I went downstairs.

Wang Yu, far removed from the previous evening's drunken and emotional state, was busy preparing an elaborate breakfast with his usual affected demeanour and nerve-racking gravity.

"Wang Yu?" I asked. "Wang Yu, was another messenger boy killed last night or early this morning?"

"I wouldn't suppose so at all," he said condescendingly. He loathed me for having seen him drunk and teary-eyed. "I was wondering what you would like for breakfast?" he asked me. "A chicken sandwich or pâté; orange juice or tea?"

I only just restrained myself from saying, "Your head, Wang Yu," and, grabbing my trench coat, I burst out into the street. There was nothing in the City Newspaper. The dear, sweet messenger boy hadn't been murdered. When I reached the office block, rather than climb up the stairs as I usually did, I planted myself in the antique elevator. Above its iron door was an exquisitely engraved depiction of Icarus, soaring and happy, heedless of his melting wings. Until that moment, I hadn't been aware of such beauty, and I was standing in amazement when I heard the sound of footsteps from behind. They got closer and closer until they stopped by my side. I saw then, they were the silver cowboy boots. Unable to raise my eyes from the sight of them, my heart pounded like mad.

"Good day! Good day!" said a bass voice. "I've been wanting to run into you for quite some time. I am Professor Domanya."

So, that imposing burly man with fat cheeks and askew brown eyes, wearing a black cloak, a huge black hat, and silver cowboy boots was the famous Professor Domanya! Like everyone else in the city, I, too, knew the whole top floor of the building (unlike the premises of all the other lawyers in the office building whose offices consisted of one or two rooms at the most) belonged to that extraordinary attorney of maritime law, Professor Domanya. Among all the myriad branches of law, maritime law is the most important to our city and Professor Domanya is its most important exponent. Once, in Monsieur Jacob's shop the conversation had turned to Professor Domanya. Monsieur Jacob had described his proficiency in his field as being "like a child who excels at marbles". "You cannot imagine, you cannot imagine," he had said, gesturing with his right hand.

With his thick, flowing voice, Professor Domanya said, "Your grandfather was my esteemed mentor. I was very pleased to hear you had started using the office. As your grandfather often used to say: 'A Stavrogin always exudes the air of the oceans.' Believe me, you changed the atmosphere of the whole office building as soon as you set foot in the place. That's the Stavrogins for you!

They bring the ocean breeze even to the most unexciting of places, I thought to myself!"

Our family's success was due entirely to its servants, I reflected as we entered the elevator. Professor Domanya planted his slightly askew eyes on mine and said, "Come to my office today. If you're as fond of the liquid delights as your grandfather was, there'll be a nice surprise awaiting you."

Could it be that this was the glove-stomping, silver-cowboy boot-wearing man who, in my dream, had inspired me with such terror? Professor Domanya was the kindest, most pleasant person I'd encountered since getting mixed up in this sordid business.

The elevator stopped on the third floor. Professor Domanya said, "The other day my goddaughter Esme dropped by your office. The hussy hasn't been seen in public since!"

Esme? His goddaughter? I was so flabbergasted that I didn't even have the presence of mind to wish him good day (or salute him with any other prosaic phrase as one ought). Thank goodness you don't have to say much of anything in response to Professor Domanya.

"Goodbye, goodbye! I'll be waiting for you today," he shouted. But then he didn't actually shout. His voice was so powerful it wrapped itself around you like an echo in a deep valley.

Professor Domanya was Esme's godfather! I hurried down the stairs and went into the little store opposite the office building. "A bottle of Johnny Walker Black Label," I said to the child behind the counter.

I was half-way through the bottle when my office door opened without a knock. She entered. She was wearing a very tight but unrevealing black dress, sheer black stockings, and high-heeled suede shoes, and over her shoulder hung a small quilted leather bag with a chain strap. Her hair was loose and unkempt. It was obvious the heavy makeup from the day before had not been removed. She swayed as she walked in her high heels towards the armchair on the right. She had drunk a lot and was a mess. She was tired. But she had shown up – what else mattered?

"What are we calling lies?" she asked. That strange, singular voice reverberated. "For the Indians there are no lies because this world isn't real. It's a tortuous, absurd place through which we come and go until we achieve liberation. We live in such an absurd world, with so many absurd regulations – whether they are called lies, truths, early, late, appropriate or inappropriate! You got angry with me because I was late. It would have been more 'appropriate' if I had come yesterday and given you an explanation. You also got angry with me for telling you false numbers and for saying that Monsieur Jacob sent me. He didn't send me. But what's so important about that? Perhaps he sent me by not sending me. I no longer keep numbers and the order of things in mind. You'll never know what pains I have taken so as not to keep such things in mind. Please, oh please, don't be angry with me. Do whatever you have to do, but don't be angry. If you hadn't loved me the moment you saw me, if you'd become irritated, if you'd felt alienated – I would have accepted it. But if you love me, love me without getting angry, I beg of you. Would you give me a little whiskey?"

I filled her glass. I wasn't going to say "For goodness sake, don't drink any more," or something like that to her. I wasn't going to bring her down with threats and warnings. Life had brought Esme down enough. I was going to be generous towards her; I was always going to treat her well. But when you love someone this much, you don't have control over your feelings – not over getting angry, or being a fool.

"I'm so happy," she said. Her eyes were brimming over with tears. She couldn't contain herself any longer; she was shaking and she started to cry. "You know that messenger boy funeral I went to? Apparently, it wasn't my son. My son is a totally different child living in house number seven. I always went to house numbers three and four, since I'd guessed my sons lived there. The City Council warned me twice about the matter. Even so, I refused to go to houses seven and eight and others. There's this horny, horrible guy who's a member of the City Council – after the funeral I went out for a drink with him in order to get him to talk. He came through of course – the one who died apparently wasn't my son. I'm so happy . . . "

Esme started to cry once more. Such an unhappy, beautiful woman! She reminded me what a rotten place this world is. If she'd proffered a knife at that moment I would have stabbed myself. "Don't cry, Esme," I said. "I can't stand seeing so much emotion. Please don't cry. Does that mean one of your sons lived in house number seven?"

"Yeah, so it seems," she said, wiping her nose. "My little six-year-old son, the one conceived from Mr. Wolfscientist's precious sperm, apparently lived in house number seven for years. And I lied to you – whatever a lie is! I have only one son. I said I had two sons because I thought you'd trust me that much more. Most of the mothers have two sons. That's the ideal number. The very successful mothers give birth even to three. They're all such revolting women. Controlled, sharp, stern women – the ideal hens. The firmament of the City Council was shaken when I became a messenger boy mother. For the first time they were confronted with a problem mother; and, of course, a second offer of motherhood didn't come my way. Of all the mothers, I also have the honour of receiving the lowest salary. They even make deductions from my salary. As for the others, those award-winning, egg-laying chickens, they even receive bonuses! If you were ever there on visiting day you wouldn't believe your eyes. They come dressed for the part, and in the most theatrical manner, they perform the most precious scenarios of love and compassion from the repertory of mother-hood – each and every one of them. Questions like, which one is mine? which one is hers? who are the fathers? who are these children?, don't even cross their minds. You would not believe it! The children are very unhappy, very depressed, and now they're being murdered one by one!"

Esme tried to hold back her tears. She put one hand over her nose and tried to cover her eyes with the other. I understood that she was deeply pained over the messenger boys. My dream came to mind.

"It seems that Professor Domanya is your godfather," I said.

"Hmmm," she said distractedly. "He was my father's closest friend. Whatever you do, though, don't tell him I came to see you today. I don't want him to see me in this state; I won't call on him. Uncle Domanya doesn't know I drink this much."

Uncle Domanya! Silver-booted Uncle Domanya! He knew she drank. Her insides were covered with wounds, unhealed wounds. And by drinking, she only poured salt on her wounds. But then, who among us doesn't?

"It's time for me to go home," she said. "I've been out two nights running – look, I'm still wearing my funeral clothes." She stopped, her eyes fixed on the empty glass in her hand. "Tomorrow I'll go and find my son," she said determinedly. "I'll definitely find my son."

"Take care of yourself, Esme," I said. At that moment she was the person I loved most in that city.

She pushed her hair back and showed me the satanic sapphire eyes encrusted over the innocent, laughing face of Murugan. "Look, I made an earring out of your key-chain. Anyway, I don't carry keys," she said.

"Murugan looks good on your ear," I said.

"Last night I lost the Bogart magazine," she said.

"That's okay," I replied.

"Alright," she said. "Goodbye, my angel," she smiled. "You also take care – you've managed to down half the bottle."

My angel? That was the first time someone had called me "my angel". She pulled the door open and left.

<hr />

Once she had left, I felt incredibly lonely. My stomach burned pitilessly from not having eaten anything all morning, from drinking whiskey, and from the excitement of seeing her. In any case, my insides were churning with an inexplicable feeling of distress and a deep sense of guilt. In spite of being wrapped up in the affair for six days, I was still only striking at thin air. You could find me guilty of pointless babble and even of being good for nothing except hitting the bottle. You could also charge me with bias and allowing my affections to get in the way. I suppose I, too, accused myself of these things. But, oh reader, I was in deep! My soul was in upheaval and my mind was set on the matter. Climbing the stairs to Professor Domanya's office I was suspicious of everyone, myself included. Everyone who had crossed my path since the beginning of this saga could be a murderer. Yet, who is not capable of being a murderer? This question was bothering me.

I reached the top of the stairs and faced Professor Domanya's black lacquer door. A lawyer who went around in silver cowboy boots would naturally have his office door painted in black lacquer, with a golden Chinese dragon embossed on it. A darkly beautiful secretary opened the door. The office had thick, wine-coloured carpet and was crammed with all manner of gilded and embossed objects. With their endearing tastelessness, they somehow put one at ease. Professor Domanya had his back to me. The wall behind his desk was covered with volumes upon volumes of law books. He was kneeling down, searching for something in a small opening in the midst of this incredible library. When I got closer I saw that he was looking in some kind of shoe rack filled with hundreds of pairs of cowboy boots in an array of colours – beige, red, black, silver and duck-green. He had taken the silver pair off and was evidently searching for a change.

"You got me! You caught me red-handed in my secret shoe cellar!" he said in that strong voice brimming with merriment. "Sit down, have a seat, please. I thought I'd change my silver boots as I've been invited to a formal dinner this evening. These, really, are no better than the other ones!"

He was gesturing at the duck-green patent leather boots on his feet. You couldn't say he was wrong; they all had pretty much the same effect.

"Ah, my passion for boots! But isn't it true, don't we exist in this world to the extent that our passions do? What are we without our passions? Your grandfather, your dearest grand-father, was a man of such passions, such passions! He often used to say, 'Stavrogins are the prisoners of their passions because they know that true captivity is the state of people without passion.' I hope I'm not being tactless in considering you a Stavrogin. If I'm not mistaken, like me, you also use your mother's surname."

"Exactly, Professor Domanya," I said. "Consider me a Stavrogin."

"To converse with your grandfather was one of the greatest pleasures in the world. You felt your heart beating and your brain cells working. He died when you were a child, didn't he? What a pity, what a great pity. I would have liked you to have heard these discussions as much as I'd like everyone to have read Dostoyevsky . . . Now tell me, what would you like to drink?"

His slightly askew brown eyes were glistening and warm. His head was quite bald; his face wide and round. I didn't have to answer him because he burst into laughter. His laughter gave you confidence. It had a quality that made you feel good inside. A prince of self-confidence, I thought to myself – not a false, heavy kind of self-confidence, but a more relaxing kind that gave you peace of mind. You felt secure on his turf, as if he would protect you and love you with his singular, soothing heart.

"Ah, don't mind my questions" he said amidst his laughter. "I prepared your drink ages ago: a wonderful cognac, your grand-father's favourite. Exactly fifty-three years old! Unfortunately, I was never able to offer him one this old; in those days I wasn't such a famous lawyer. I was just a young punk. We once had a bet and I lost. I could never buy such a priceless cognac as this. The cognac we drank was only seventeen years old, but he didn't reproach me for it at all. He was a very refined person. He knew about liquor, he knew about people; in short, your grandfather knew about life. Now the world is crawling with people who go around saying, 'I don't understand life, life perplexes me.' As if they'd done anything to understand life! As if to understand life they'd bothered to get up from their armchairs!"

Professor Domanya had become angry and was revealing a totally different side of his personality. He shoved the boot rack with his hand and it revolved round to complete the library shelves once again. Professor Domanya's taste in clothes and decor was really quite surprising. His face was also quite surprising when he got angry; in a flash he could resemble a wicked Indian god.

He filled our glasses — let my stomach burn! I drew in the aroma of the marvellous fifty-three-year-old cognac. "Why did you enter into a bet with my grandfather, Professor Domanya?" I asked in curiosity.

He replied: "You know your grandfather returned to India when he was fifty years old. At the peak of his career, he suddenly closed his office door and returned to Bombay were he'd grown up. It's funny, it seems that those who go to India never come back; and if they do, a part of them stays there forever. Yet, for him to suddenly get up and leave everything behind really surprised us all. 'Don't go,' I said to him. 'If you go you'll never come back again to our city.' 'I bet you I'll come back to our city,' he told me. 'Don't worry, I'll come back. This is just a break.' That was how we came to have a bet over this cognac. We were all astonished when, three years later, he returned with a scrawny Indian kid. He returned to the city, but he never returned to his practice. For seventeen years, until his death, he went back and forth to his office — to get out of the house, to drink his booze, to read his movie magazines. So, in a sense I won the bet: you couldn't say your grandfather came back from India. Now as for that Indian child, he was a weird one; he was like your grandfather's shadow. He was like a sick, pathetic puppy dog. He shivered from head to toe if he wasn't by your grandfather's side."

"Wang Yu?" I said, my voice ringing with astonishment.

"Yes, yes! Your grandfather had given him just such a weird Chinese name. Wang Yu! Yes, such a pathetic child."

Pathetic Indian child! Pathetic Wang Yu! I was no longer in any condition to take in life's bizarre surprises and was about to faint. What was so special about Wang Yu that made my grandfather carry him back from India as though he were a suitcase — what was his secret?

My glass was empty. I got up and politely bade Professor Domanya farewell. "Esme visited you today," he said, just as I was about to leave his room and as if it had just crossed his mind. "The hussy didn't drop by to see me! She drinks so much she's ruining herself. I'm very worried about her. Messenger boy motherhood has made my lovely one so wretched."

I saw an inexpressible sorrow in his eyes. It was evident how much he loved Esme.

"Goodbye, Professor Domanya," I said once more. "Thank you for the cognac. It's the best I've ever had."

"You're always welcome. Please come again."

"Goodbye," I said for the third time. "So long, Professor Domanya."

I ran down the stairs and walked home so fast that I arrived out of breath. Wang Yu was sitting in the kitchen reading his newspaper. He had prepared my favourite meal of Chinese rice with shrimp, almond chicken, and peach compote.

"Would you join me for supper tonight, Wang Yu?" I asked. "As you know, I don't like eating alone."

"Alright, if you wish," said Wang Yu, and his face showed his thanks for the honour. Alright, so be it! I opened a bottle of red wine.

"To your honour," I toasted Wang Yu. "Or as the Japanese say: *Kampai!*"

"*Kampai*," said Wang Yu. He smiled as if everything, starting with life, was a sham. Even his smile resembled my mother's.

And even if he didn't actually dislike me, he didn't enjoy sharing my mother with me, I reflected.

After supper, as was my habit to relax my nerves, I went to my room to study the collection of seashells spread out on the round mahogany table. They'd been collected from the shores of Karachi, Goa, Penang. Suddenly there was a knock at the door and Wang Yu stuck in his head. "There's a messenger boy waiting for you downstairs," he said.

It was well past midnight and I was alarmed. "Bring him up here immediately, Wang Yu," I said. "What could be happening at this hour of the night?"

When Wang Yu brought him in, I couldn't believe my eyes. No messenger boy stood in front of me, instead it seemed as though a street child who'd been kicked off some Hollywood film set stood there. Instead of the messenger boys' habitually starched and pure white sleeves, his lace cuffs were torn and filthy as if he had been rubbing his arms on the walls. His curly blond locks looked like they hadn't been washed for days. There was lipstick on his cheeks as if he'd just been kissed by some loving lady.

"I've brought you a message," he said holding out a small envelope.

My name was written in a messy and hurried hand. With my heart pounding, I asked, "Is this from Esme?"

"Uh-huh," he said in a distracted, nonchalant manner.

I thought to myself that no messenger boy would ever answer anyone like that. Without a doubt, this was the messenger boy I'd sent the other day to Esme and Mr. Wolfscientist – the one with mud splashed the back of his sock! And who did his 'uh-huh' remind me of? Why Esme of course! This had to be Esme's son; he was different from the other messenger boys.

"How old are you, messenger boy," I asked in excitement.

"I'm six years old," he said, his eyes fixed on the shells on the table.

"What's the number of the messenger boy house you live in?"

"Number seven," he answered.

I thought to myself that he wasn't a messenger boy at all – just a boy. Esme's son! How he loved those seashells. I gathered them all up and put them in their velvet bag.

"Here, have them," I said. "I'll collect some more another time."

"But sir! Those shells may well be from the shores of Pakistan, India, and Malaysia. And – I beg your pardon – in any case messenger boys cannot accept gifts. But it's very kind of you, very, very kind of you."

He seemed about to cry. It occurred to me that his soul seemed to fluctuate between that of a messenger boy's and a child's. He was in torment, restless, unhappy. Just like Esme.

"Please accept these shells," I said. "When you are feeling low you can look at them. Believe me, they make a person relax."

A person? Messenger boys were people too. Even though they

were the crowning achievement of genetic engineering, even though they were flawless, they were also people, children, human. So, did Esme know? Did she know that this darling child was her son?

"Could you please wait a moment," I asked. "I want to read this letter and send an answer with you."

"Of course, sir," he said. By now he'd taken the velvet bag.

The dear child couldn't refuse the shells! I wanted to hug him and toss him up in the air. I quickly ripped open the envelope and read the letter:

> *I'm in a panic. Okay, I'll get right to the truth. I'm fright-ened. I wanted to let you know so I sat down and am writ-ing this in a rush. Today they actually tried to kill me. After leaving your office I went home. I was very tired. I was knocked out with sleep. I could have gone on sleeping forever . . . There's a very sweet old woman in the flat across the hall who I leave my keys with and so on. She noticed the smell of gas coming from my flat, tried to force open the door and couldn't. She broke down the door and came in to find the gas turned on and the cracks in the win-dows and doors stuffed with rags. This business definitely has something to do with the City Council and a certain matter about which you can guess. I'm writing this from a friend's house. Don't reply. Tomorrow I'll drop by, we'll talk about it. Take care of yourself!*
>
> *Love, Esme*

They had tried to kill her for trying to find her son. The City Council, the messenger boy murders . . .

"May I go," he asked.

"Yes, yes, you go on," I said. But a second later, in sudden panic, I said, "No, stay here. Hey, don't you know that messenger boys — " I was almost shouting.

He smiled very sweetly. "Don't worry," he said. "It's expressly forbidden for messenger boys to stay anywhere other than messenger boy houses. I wish you a good night, sir. Thank you very much for the shells."

He quickly left. I was about to go crazy. Esme . . . her son . . . the mysterious murderers turning on the gas and stuffing all the cracks with rags. The City Council, the messenger boy murders . . . I thought I wouldn't sleep a wink that night. I was wrong. Ten minutes after the messenger boy left, I was sleeping like a lamb.

When I awoke it was in the wee hours of the morning. Outside it was drizzling. I had slept without interruption; I couldn't recall any of my dreams. My heart, however, was as light as a bird; I must have been dreaming of pleasant things. No matter what, we always remember our bitter, sorrowful dreams. As if it isn't enough to disturb us in our sleep, they pass in front of our eyes like a reel of film and tear our insides apart when we wake. Pleasant dreams are the most difficult to remember: they lighten our hearts, they awaken us to good mornings; yet they won't come out into the open.

I quickly got dressed. I pressed my grandfather's trench coat under my arm and went softly down the stairs. I didn't want to have breakfast or see Wang Yu. I was full of joy and couldn't contain myself. With the trench coat still under my arm I got lightly rained on as I made my way straight to the office building. If I'm not mistaken, I think I even whistled. From the store at the corner I got a tuna fish sandwich and a glass of jasmine tea. I thought that this was the beauty of living in a port city. I don't remember now why this crossed my mind but it definitely did.

In the office building, Icarus greeted me from above the iron door of the elevator. My grandfather's office seemed to me old and noble. "Old and noble, not like me," I told myself.

I was seated at my table eating my sandwich and drinking my tea when there was a gentle knock at the door. "Come in," I responded. "The door's open, please do come in!"

"Please, don't get up, don't get up," he said as he entered. As I guessed, it was my neighbour from the third floor — the gentleman who paid me a visit once before and had spouted praise for Wang Yu.

I leapt out of my seat and motioned to the armchair on the left: "Please, make yourself at home," I said. I'm one who believes that if you're in a good frame of mind there's no reason not to be polite.

"Amazing," he said. "You're never one to come early in the morning."

He was very thin and old. His hair was pure white. As for his hands, they were covered with veins and almost blue. It occurred to me that when he was young he was probably a redhead. Don't ask what made me think this. If we'd met around a drinking table I would certainly have asked him, but this time I declined to ask that old and distinguished gentleman anything. Instead, I respectfully waited for him to bring up the subject.

"I came by to tell you about Wang Yu's secret," he said. "I thought you might be curious about it."

I remember my two hands gripping the sides of my chair. I gripped so hard that my palms were still sore the next day.

"Or perhaps, to say, 'we thought . . .' might be more correct. That is, Jacob and I thought . . . "

He stopped; he weighed every phrase in a delicate balance. "This is amazing," I said to myself, "An old, distinguished, gentleman who weighs his words with care has come to tell me about the secret of Wang Yu!"

"Yesterday evening I dropped by Jacob's. Occasionally I call on him; he's a very dear, old friend of mine. He's a tremendous individual, a venerable gentleman, a marvellous bookseller."

I bit my lip so as not to shriek out: "He's the cause of all that has happened or is going to happen to me!" I held myself back with great difficulty.

"You know us old folks – one topic leads to another, and we ended up talking about you. And therefore we thought you'd be curious about Wang Yu's secret."

I couldn't control myself any longer. "Yes, sir," I said. "In this sometimes discrete, sometimes garrulous, maddeningly unpredictable city, this is the subject that piques my curiosity the most." I was becoming impulsive; I immediately shut up.

"I sincerely encourage you to avoid things that are easily understood," he said. "Sometimes things that are easily understood don't even deserve to be understood. Moreover, there are things so easily understood that a thoughtful and deep person's mind can be blurred by their facility. This is because such mind looks for more depth in everything than there actually is. Besides, let's not be unfair to our city, young friend; our city is one of the world's oldest and most beautiful urban labyrinths. Not that I didn't think when I was young, passionate, and rebellious like you that the only way out of this city was through the seas surrounding it! But this complicated city, this city you accuse of being maddening – it is a city that breathes and keeps people alive."

He smiled softly. There's something about the smile of women and the old that makes one melt and makes what they say seem believable.

"You're quite right," I said looking straight ahead, "you're so right, sir."

"Coming to Wang Yu's secret," he said. "He was a hijra."

"A hijra?" I said.

"No, you did not hear wrong," he said. "When Wang Yu was eleven years old he ran away from his village in Maharashtra and went to New Delhi. When his mother died his relatives in the village mistreated him, pushed him around . . . Instead of going to the nearest big city – that is instead of going to Bombay – he wanted to escape to a city as far away as possible. He arrived in New Delhi after a journey fraught with suffering. There, on his first day, the unfortunate child fell into the hands of the hijras. They fed him and quenched his thirst; even let him ride on the carousel. He awoke that night in incredible agony; the hijras who had castrated him were surrounding him like vultures, shrieking in jubilation at the new member in their midst. Clearly he was a child of delicate, sensitive spirit; he never forgot that scene, that night of dread. For three or four months he fluttered helplessly but didn't have the chance to escape. During this time he learned to dance and sing songs at weddings. This work was very onerous for him; twice he tried to kill himself. Finally, an old hijra took pity on him and arranged his escape. Wang Yu took refuge in that city he'd been too afraid to go to on leaving his village: Bombay. But he was so affected by what he'd been through that when your grandfather found him in the streets he was close to death. Your grandfather looked after him for months and stayed at his side through nights of nightmare. To amuse and console him your grandfather bought him a Madagascan crow. He taught him our language. But, two years later, when it came time for your grandfather to return to our city, the poor little one begged him not to leave him behind. He wanted to be his servant – he cried that he had no other desire in life than that. This servant idea didn't sit well with your grandfather. 'What would I do with a servant like you! The servants you're talking about are Chinese, like in the novels – they have names like "Wang Yu" and so forth. In any case, you know I'm not the kind of man to have or take pleasure in having a servant,' he said. The little one became fixated on the name. 'From now on my name is Wang Yu,' he insisted, 'and I am your servant.' Your grandfather was stuck in the proverbial creek, yet he couldn't bear to leave him behind, to break his heart. He returned to our city with a servant he had acquired through obligation. So there, that's Wang Yu's secret! Also, as you know, he's madly in love with your mother. When your mother was leaving home as a young bride he sank his teeth in the door. Your grandfather used to say that no repair or paint job was capable of covering up those tooth marks. Ah, what love! You should have seen Wang Yu's eyes when your father passed away seven years later and your mother returned to your grandfather's house . . . He's a uniquely proud person. He performs his work perfectly. And, he's one of our city's most important authorities on Shakespeare. On certain evenings of the month, at meetings held in Jacob's shop, he recites Shakespeare to us and gives commentaries."

Such is Wang Yu's secret, oh inquisitive reader!

The old gentleman evidently became tired after telling the story, since he made a move to leave.

"Please, allow me, I'm much obliged," I said showing him to the door.

When I returned to my grandfather's desk, my legs were shaking with excitement from having heard Wang Yu's story. Dear Wang Yu, I thought to myself. Dear, dear, dear Wang Yu!

From excitement or sorrow I sink easily into exhaustion: I become sleepy. Wang Yu's story had this affect on me. Not five minutes after I bade farewell to the gentleman, I stretched out on my table and went fast asleep.

In my dream five or six hijras in silk saris, bejewelled, their faces painted layer upon layer, were screaming in their high-pitched voices and twirling around in front of the door of a house where a wedding was being held. At a window on the second floor of the house the curtains were gently parted; a girl with white complexion and blue eyes looked down on them in horror. One of the hijras noticed the little girl; he raised his huge, henna-decorated hand, pointing her out to the others. They all raised their hands simultaneously to point at the girl. Then they began dancing the "cursed bride" dance that would damn her for the rest of her life. At first, the little girl sobbed. After a while, though, she opened the windows wide and threw whatever came to hand at the hijras: lace, picture frames, an inkpot, and so on. Lastly, she hurled a porcelain doll at the head of the oldest hijra and, by some amazing coincidence, hit him. Blood began to flow from the old hijra's head and all the other hijras gathered around him, fluttering. A crooked smile crossed the little girl's otherwise beautiful face and she began to shout out: "Esme. My name's Esme! Esme!"

I was woken by knocking at the door. Actually, it was something between knocking and an attempt at breaking down the door: the Irish-Cap-Man had arrived.

"Are you s-s-sleeping like that again?" he asked. He started to laugh.

"Oh no," I thought to myself. "The stuttering, shouting, spitting, laughing – that tiring man again . . . Why does he have to show up all the time?!"

Settling into the armchair he threw his legs over the sides and said, "Getting down to the reason for my visit . . . I've brought your magazine back."

He pulled an old movie magazine out of the inside pocket of his overcoat and tossed it in front of me. He was right. It was the magazine that Esme said she had lost – the one with Humphrey Bogart on the cover.

"Do you mind if I ask where you found that magazine?" I said.

"I don't mind at all, really, I don't mind," he said with difficulty and launched into such a fit of laughter that I was filled with dread.

The Irish-Cap-Man seemed to find humour in the most unexpected words. To talk with him was like strolling through a field sown with laughter mines. It was utterly impossible to predict when and which one of your words would set off an explosion.

His laughter turned to sobbing. He must have noticed the sour expression on my face, because he calmed down and suddenly looked crestfallen. There, now his heart was broken. Without a doubt he was thinking, "Another robot!" From time to time I may be capable of being bad-hearted, but somehow I've never succeeded in being stonehearted. I was so upset over hurting his feelings that I couldn't keep my voice from quivering.

"Actually, my good man," I said, "I wanted to say this: I'd already given that magazine to that lady I'd mentioned. The one who is keen on Humphrey Bogart . . . So, seeing you with it . . . "

He softened up. His eyes were shining like a puppy dog's. "Come on, can you guess where I found this magazine?" he quizzed. "In a drinking den where only dwarves work! Come on, guess its name. Can you guess the name of that dump?"

"It must be *Snow White*," I said, trying to balance distance and affection.

"No!" he shouted. "It's *The Cave*."

"I get it," I said. "I get it."

A lump settled in my throat. What kind of places did Esme hang out in? What kind of people did she drink with? Who knows where else she could have gone – aside from that "dump" called *The Cave*. Those two nights running when she didn't go home that she'd mentioned with that tight mourning dress on . . . and above all with whom? . . . and she hadn't shown up today . . . and she probably wouldn't. She'd forget all about the letter she'd sent me last night. Who knows where and with whom she would be drinking as she forgot about me, her son, the messenger boys, and herself? My bitterness and sorrow suddenly turned into an insane rage. If she had come through the door at that moment I could have attacked her; I could have hurled the heaviest insults that came to my mind. I could even have walked up to her and struck her twice.

Oh reader, the transformation from sorrow to rage is that most direct but illogical path known as jealousy! There is no equal to that ugly, contagious feeling that makes you lose your self-esteem, that makes you battle dangerously with yourself. It grows over the site of one's passion like a shameless weed and wraps itself around the soul, and while your soul struggles breathlessly for life, that shameless plant grows bigger and stronger. It drives you mad, then it annihilates you. Protect your soul: beware of jealousy, ambition — remember that the threat of annihilation at any moment may be at your door!

As for me, at that moment I was about to drown from rage, passion, and jealousy. Thank god the Irish-Cap-Man was there, or I might have. In that state, even the presence of one of the sources of my rage could save me from it.

"I had to resign from my job," he said. "N-n-now, whether I want to or not, I'm going to have to get into an academic career. I'm g-g-going back to university. How's that! Good, don't you think?"

"So, you were fired?" I asked.

"In a way," he replied, smothering his laughter. "I was forced to resign. I spoke about what happened to me on that business trip. Because of those people at the fair — "

He didn't finish his sentence. One hand tried to wipe away the tears streaming from his eyes, while the other clutched at his belly.

The ugly clouds hovering over my soul were dispelled. My dream came to mind. Esme was cursed. She was very beautiful, special, and very unfortunate. Suddenly my insides were awash in a marvellous wave of love and compassion. "I wish I'd met her as a little girl!" I thought to myself. It's easier for us to love people when they are children. Was it easier? I don't know. What I did know was that I couldn't get Esme out of my mind.

"It's time I was g-g-going," he said.

"Your mother?" I asked.

"Noooo," he said. "I don't have to be anywhere today. I just want to leave at an appropriate time."

"Goodbye," I said. "Take care of yourself."

He rose to his feet, but he was bent double with laughter.

"You use such funny words!" he said. "You amuse me so much."

"The feeling is mutual," I said.

He was still shaking with laughter as he went out the door. He was laughing so hard it seemed as though the stairs shook.

Once the Irish-Cap-Man left, I was overcome with the feeling that I couldn't contain myself. I thought I could hear the fluttering wings of birds of anticipation. I thought that I couldn't bear to stay there any longer. I jumped up from my table, snatched the trench coat and went outside. I walked through the city's winding streets. When I arrived home, Wang Yu's eyes said everything: my mother had returned from the summer house.

"Your esteemed mother has prepared a magnificent meal for you. I believe she also left you a note and went to sleep. She was so, so tired . . . "

I couldn't keep my eyes from searching for those tooth marks left on the doorframe. My esteemed mother returning from the summer house, tiring herself out preparing food, and falling asleep as if she were a child exhausted from play seemed the most wonderful thing in the world to Wang Yu. He was gripped by that feeling for whatever my mother did. So, that was love! Love was addiction; it was difficult.

My mother's note was on the mahogany table. In her almost indecipherable handwriting she had written:

> *I have prepared some delicious food for you! Enjoy it. I'm more tired than words can say, so I'm going to bed.*

> *With regret, your mother*

Whatever the case, I didn't feel like going downstairs to eat my precious mother's food under the gaze of Wang Yu. I made a chicken sandwich and retired to my room. One way or another, I knew I had reached the end of this business — I felt that the mystery of the messenger boy murders was about to resolve itself. But that didn't make me feel any happier; on the contrary, I felt depressed. Probably because Esme hadn't come by to see me that day. Allowing your happiness to depend on one person is always the greatest of torments. That's why Wang Yu had suffered for years. I'd had enough of mulling over what love may or may not be and decided to read Andersen's *Fairy Tales*.

I settled into one of the deep-red armchairs and had just taken the book in hand when there was a knock at the door. Wang Yu came in, his eyes revealing that even he had started to get worried. "A messenger boy again," he said. "He has apparently brought you some very important news."

"I'll be down immediately, Wang Yu," I said. "Tell him to wait for me." I put on a sweater and hung the trench coat over my arm. I knew that night I was going to be summoned somewhere.

Even the messenger boy awaiting me downstairs was alarmed. Recently, the messenger boys had changed; they expressed their delight, their anger, their panic. I suspect that they had started to feel such emotions for the first time. As my beloved grandfather had once written in a letter: *There is no emotion that isn't shown; only indifference can be hidden. In life, what could be easier than this — to hide something that doesn't exist!*

"Monsieur Jacob sent me," he said. "He requests that you go to his shop immediately."

"I'm leaving this instant, messenger boy," I said. "Look, I have my trench coat under my arm."

"Please, sir," he said.

"Yes, messenger boy," I replied.

"It's nothing, nothing," he said. He dashed out and was gone.

I thought to myself that this was the first time a departing messenger boy hadn't said goodbye. Something was going on with the messenger boys. Without a doubt something we hadn't understood, something we hadn't even tried to understand.

I sped out of the house and by the time I reached Monsieur Jacob's shop I was out of breath. Monsieur Jacob was in the back of the shop sitting in his rocking chair. He was in a wretched state.

"Monsieur Jacob," I said. "Monsieur Jacob, what's wrong, what's happened?"

"He has been killed, the poor dear," he said. "Another messenger boy has been murdered. What's more, this is the crudest of all: a murder in the guise of a suicide! I can't stand it . . . I can't stand it anymore. For goodness sake, do something, do something!" he said. Shaking like a leaf, he began to cry.

The worst punishment for me was to see Monsieur Jacob rocking to-and-fro in his chair, quivering in tears. I felt like someone who has been condemned to perpetual isolation. This time, Monsieur Jacob's tears didn't make me feel sorrow, compassion, helplessness, but only and solely this sensation: the feeling that in that shop, in that city, on this planet, I was utterly alone. I waited for his crying to stop.

"He hanged himself right in our courtyard, in the plane tree in the old booksellers' courtyard. Or, that's what we assumed at first. We figured that he had committed suicide. You'd met him as well. He was the oldest of the messenger boys – Nicholai.

Apparently, they call each other by the names of beloved heroes from novels they read. Had you ever thought of that?"

"I'd been thinking about it," I said. "I've been thinking about it for quite some time. They probably wouldn't call each other 478, 613, or The Messenger Boy Born on the 24th of August." I'll admit it, I was in an extremely foul mood.

"Ah," he said. "Ah! Ah! They took the body away a little while ago. To see that darling, tiny body swinging from a tree! Believe me, it was unbearable."

I had heard those words in just the same order, in just the same manner from someone else before. Where had I heard them? From Mr. Wolfscientist, of course! Which meant, for both of them to use the same phrases, Monsieur Jacob must have seen Mr. Wolfscientist quite often. And what was more, they had been hiding it from me! Perhaps the whole city was a chorus using the same words for the same events. They were seeing each other all the time, they knew what had happened and what was going to happen, but they still hid it from me. And they still expected me to solve the mystery of the messenger boy murders! That was unfair! What did they want from me — what did they want?

"How did you find out that his name was Nicholai, Monsieur Jacob?" I asked. "Of course, if you have just learned this today . . . "

"Ah!" he said. "The first one to pass by and notice the body was a messenger boy. He collapsed under the tree. 'Nicholai! Nicholai!' he was crying when we found him. Probably the corpse was brought at twilight and hung in the tree to make it appear a suicide, because when the City Doctor arrived on the scene he understood the situation immediately: Nicholai had been poisoned. Most likely he'd been dead since midnight of the night before. But who hanged him, how he was hanged, why we didn't see or notice the culprits . . . I just don't know. It must have been because of the darkness, the drizzle and so on.

Anyway, most of the shops were already closed. I hadn't closed up my shop because late tonight there was going to be a Shakespeare meeting. As my gracious friend, your gentleman neighbour has related to you, our friend Wang Yu was going to recite passages and offer his interpretation of *A Midsummer Night's Dream.*"

"Oh really?" I said, "As you so correctly observed, I just learned this morning from my gentleman neighbour that Wang Yu is our city's most renowned Shakespeare expert. Had I known this before I, too, might have wanted to benefit from his erudition, seeing as we live in the same house . . . "

"My young friend," said Monsieur Jacob. "My young friend, you are impatient. Don't allow life's secrets to infuriate you; because what makes life beautiful, what makes life precious is our secrets. Wait, and life will open its secrets one by one in front of you. That's not to say that when I was young I didn't rebel like you."

"Yes, Monsieur Jacob," I said, interrupting him. "And I'm willing to bet that you thought the only way out of this city was by the seas that surround it!"

Jacob's old body shook as he laughed. "You're so observant," he said. "And so suspicious. What lovely virtues! Only, if you don't adjust their dose, those virtues may poison you. Yes, my young friend, over time close friends' speech begins to resemble each other. They aren't even able to distinguish who said which word, nor would they want to. They reach the state of being the translator of each others' feelings; their points of view coincide; their thoughts coincide; their words coincide; they can easily express each others' feelings. I hope that someday you too will have such close, such precious friends."

"Would you think me unvirtuous if I said that I found this city's circle of friendships dangerous?"

"Yes! Yes! Yes, my young friend!" interjected Monsieur Jacob.

"Your extreme suspicion sometimes prevents you from seeing the whole picture. You get swamped in the details. You get fed up with the details that you see with your magnifying glass, yet you fail to step back and view the picture as a whole. Details are tedious, but the whole is enlightening."

"Monsieur Jacob," I said, "a while ago you accused me of wandering around the ground floor of the building. You claimed that if I got out on the roof I'd see everything. Somehow, I have this feeling that the moment I come out onto the roof I'm going to be pushed straight off by mysterious hands. What would you say to that?"

"The messenger boy murders," he said. "Don't forget: If anyone can, you'll solve this case."

"Once you sent Nicholai to me," I said. "He was strikingly ill-tempered."

"He was unhappy," said Jacob. "He was intelligent, aware of life."

"Goodnight, Monsieur Jacob," I said. "It appears that tonight your Shakespeare meeting isn't going to take place. In any case my mother has returned from the summer house. By now Wang Yu has probably begun to see several midsummer night dreams of his own."

"Goodnight, young friend," said Monsieur Jacob. "Your tongue is sharp, your intelligence awake. Take care of yourself, for goodness sake."

"At least this is a city of rhymes," I said. "The world is full of so many rhyme-less, unpoetic cities! Again, goodnight."

I left the shop and walked quickly. I hadn't gone more than two or three hundred meters when I spied the Irish-Cap-Man on the opposite sidewalk. He was trying to button up his trousers as he walked along and was so absorbed in this operation that he hadn't even noticed me. I turned back and began following him. He turned into one street, then another until he stopped in front of an old building. He adjusted his cap and went down the winding stairway at the side of the building. At the top of the stairs I stopped and looked down. On an iron door, in red spray paint, was written:

THE CAVE

Beneath this, in squiggly letters was written:

First enters Ahab, then everyone else

When I got home, I was met with silence and darkness; Wang Yu must have been asleep. Generally, Wang Yu didn't sleep until late; he didn't turn off the lights in his room until two or three in the morning. Knowing that he rose early, I had been wondering what kept him so busy till so late at night. But now, of course, I knew the answer: Wang Yu was reading Shakespeare over and over, preparing lectures that would satisfy the pedantic students who awaited him with baited breath at the meetings in Monsieur Jacob's shop. But tonight the words I had expended on Monsieur Jacob with my sharp tongue turned out to be true. He had gone to bed early in honour of my mother's return. I drew a sigh of relief. My mind was in such a tangle, my insides so agitated that I was in no state to see anyone or to endure even the most superficial of social interactions.

I entered my room and sat down on one of the chairs at the round mahogany table. On a piece of parchment paper I wrote:

Dear Mr. Wolfscientist,

    I'm quite certain that you are far from being one of Monsieur Jacob's "new" customers. I am filled with suspicion as to why this fact has been hidden from me . . .

This is not the first fact that you have hidden from me. When I learned that you were one of our city's reputable sperm-sellers you warned me in a "friendly" manner. You warned me against drawing conclusions before fully grasping a subject, and against taking an accusatory approach. The pieces of the puzzle before me do not add up. I've had it. I want to run away from this city. I ask you bluntly: Are you the murderer?

P.S. And anyway, what are these murders to me?

I filled the glass on my bedside table with whiskey. As if dying from thirst, I tilted back my head and drank, and drank, and drank . . . "Anyway, what are these murders to me?" I reflected on that extraordinary phrase. I filled up my glass, and on another piece of white parchment wrote:

Esme,

> *Aside from the fact that you don't keep any of your promises*

I stopped. I was having difficulty holding onto my pen.

> *Alright, where are you?*

I wrote.

I went straight for my bed. Without getting undressed I lay down and fell into a deep sleep.

When I woke up it was three in the afternoon. It was Sunday. Exactly seven days had passed since I had got mixed up in this business. Feeling the fatigue of fifteen hours of sleep, I had a bath. My mother and Wang Yu, as they generally did on Sundays, had gone to the Antique Photograph Bazaar. I had a peaceful meal. I returned to my room whistling, but then — I couldn't believe my eyes — gone from the table were the letters I had written to Mr. Wolfscientist and Esme.

My mother? Wang Yu?

Which meddler could have sent those two hare-brained letters without my consent and approval? Both Wang Yu and my mother were capable of such tactlessness. I nearly had a fit. But what possessed me to sit down and write such letters, without logic and reason? Why did I write to Mr. Wolfscientist? Why did I insist on dealing with the man? As for Esme, what did I want from her? She would show up if she felt like it; she would keep her word if it suited her. Was there any point in dwelling on it?

Loathing both myself and the meddler who had sent the letters, I returned to my bed. I wasn't sleepy but I was afraid of making another gaffe. Taking a book in hand I pulled the covers over me, and ten minutes later I was sleeping like a lamb.

The next morning I awoke to Wang Yu entering my room and pulling back the curtains.

"Good morning," said Wang Yu, "I thought you might like to wake up early and head off to your grandfather's office."

"You're quite right, Wang Yu," I said. "But thank you for not addressing me as your 'young friend'."

"Since your birth I've always addressed you with due respect," said Wang Yu. "As you know I am your grandfather's servant."

"You were his servant," I said. "Whatever kind of servitude . . ."

"I chose of my own free will to be your grandfather's servant'," Wang Yu cut in. "I wish you a good day."

He went out. At that moment, I didn't have a shadow of a doubt as to who had sent those letters. Of course, he had sent them! Dear Wang Yu, I thought. Dear, dear, dear Wang Yu.

I didn't want to break Wang Yu's heart by not eating breakfast at home so I hurriedly ate something from the carefully prepared table and left. I bought a box of valium and a bottle of aspirin from the City Pharmacy directly across from the house and set off for the office. As soon as I sat down at my desk I emptied into a glass the last of the whiskey I had bought the day

Esme last visited, popped two aspirin and three valium pills into my mouth, and washed them down. I didn't want my nerves to be shaken by anything. Taking valium with whiskey may not seem like a good idea to you, but at that moment, I didn't much care. I just wanted to swallow them down, to calm and protect myself. And I was right: the door opened without a knock and in came Mr. Nerve-racking Wolfscientist.

"Unbelievable!" he said. "It really is unbelievable!"

"Coming from you, that is an unexpectedly short statement," I said. At that moment I wanted the earth to split and swallow me — anything but to talk with that flawless man about my latest fault.

"I never told you I was a 'new' customer of Monsieur Jacob's," he said. "Of course Monsieur Jacob could have said that I was. But this doesn't make me responsible for what Monsieur Jacob says, and I don't go along with this line of reasoning anyway. Time is relative, as even you may know, and it could be that all customers that he has known for less than twenty years fall into the 'new' category. Humility, tolerance, foresight, logic, caution, the placing of yourself in others' shoes — yes, yes, your most striking deficiency is this — not putting yourself in the other person's position. Such qualities haven't even gained a toe-hold in your character."

"Wouldn't you like to take a seat?" I said. "Care for a little whiskey, a few valium?"

"Whaaat!" he exclaimed as his eyes flashed with lightning. "Did you also commit that act of thoughtlessness? Hurry up and try to vomit. I beg you . . . how could you do that, how could you?"

"Don't worry," I responded. "Of course I didn't do such a thing, I merely recommended it to you." I made an effort to smile. That humourless man! Now he had taken it upon himself to save me by getting me to throw up!

He sat down in the armchair to my left and from behind his wire-framed spectacles fixed his slightly slanted eyes on mine. "No," he said, "I'm not the murderer."

Most likely he had read in an article somewhere that you are much more likely to be believed if you look straight into the eyes of the person facing you when making such a statement.

"You are convincing," I said. "And in any case, I didn't have any doubts about you. But there is something about you that inspires one to write letters. At the moment we are both the victims of that quality of yours."

Even I was surprised at my boldness and thoughtlessness.

He laughed. Yes, he burst into laughter. "When everything is this simple," he said, "how happy, how happy we are."

"How happy we are," I repeated. What a strange phrase that was!

The door opened without a knock and in came Esme. She was wearing a leather jacket, a black sweater, a pair of tight jeans, and rough leather cowboy boots. Her hair was a mess from the night before. She sat down in the armchair directly across from Mr. Wolfscientist and fixed her eyes on mine. Those beautiful eyes.

"I'm here," she said. "But where are you?"

With a sarcastic expression Mr. Wolfscientist first scrutinized her, then me. I couldn't loathe that man as much as I wanted to; there was a good side to him.

"My son, my little son is also here," she said. "I found him! He's so sweet, so, so sweet." She turned her head and planted her close-set eyes on Mr. Wolfscientist: "My son from your precious sperm," she said. "At last I know which messenger boy he is; I've found him." Then she sobbed.

Mr. Wolfscientist's eyes evaded hers. "I'm delighted for you, Ms. Esme," he said. "Yet, I hope you don't confuse normal motherhood with messenger boy motherhood. That would not only be extremely dangerous for you, but for your 'little' son as well."

"Ms. Esme isn't concerned with anything other than that she has found her son and is reunited with him, Mr. Wolfscientist," said Esme. "Neither the City Council nor the sacred institution of the messenger boys are of any concern to her. I gave birth to him and I want to save my son from that ridiculous, inhuman project. Maybe being a sperm-merchant did not awaken feelings of fatherhood in you, but since the very beginning I have partic-ipated in this disgusting game with the hope of being reunited with my son."

"You are insolent," said Mr. Wolfscientist. "You are drunk, obnoxious, and thoughtless to the extreme. You're like a child playing with fire. I want to caution you in a friendly manner."

"In a friendly manner!" shouted Esme. "What's your friend-ship worth! I don't need your wisdom or your pompous phrases. It's enough for me that I've saved my son from that wretched life. Not in the name of this or that; just because I wanted it so! Because I love my son, because I missed him! If anything gets burned it will be my own hand. I couldn't care less. How dare you preach to me! First deal with your own problems – clean up your own conscience!"

Mr. Wolfscientist rose from his armchair and said, "Good day to you both." It was clear that he thought us a marvellous couple. He was no longer in the mood to put up with us – especially with Esme. He pulled the door behind himself gently and was gone.

Men's passion for reasonable, decent women makes me nau-seous. Mr. Wolfscientist was afraid of Esme. He was afraid of her beauty, her intelligence, her drunkenness, and above all, her untamed personality. Esme was like a solitary ship at sail on a stormy sea; a black flag hung from the mast, a pirate ship terrorizing the passenger liners that drew by.

"I can't believe that man," she said. "It's time for me to go. I came to see you so that you wouldn't worry about me. I'm fine, really, I'm fine. I'm staying with a friend. I'm going to escape from this city once I've grabbed my son. I'm finishing my preparations."

"Take care, Esme," I said.

She pushed her hair back and showed me the satanic eyes imbedded in Murugan's innocent face. "While I've got this, nothing will happen to me. Don't worry, my angel," she said.

"Are your boots a present from Professor Domanya?" I asked.

"Uh-huh," she responded. "Uncle Domanya practically drowns me in gifts. They'll come in handy if I have to kick someone — look how pointed the toes are!" She demonstrated by lifting a leg.

She rose, swaying back and forth. "You look after yourself as well, my angel," she said. "Your face is like chalk."

She pulled the door open and left.

I went to the bathroom on the third floor and locked the door behind me. I leaned over the sink and puked. I puked and puked. I wanted to run away and save myself from that city.

Would you like to learn something about Lana Turner? I certainly would. After they left and I had thoroughly emptied my innards into the sink, I went back to my desk, grabbed one of the movie magazines lying in the vicinity, and started reading. Lana Turner was on the cover and, inside, there was a seven-page interview with her. In spite of my concerted effort to concentrate and the well-written and fluid dialogue, I couldn't make any sense of it — even after reading each sentence four or five times. I must have wrestled with that interview for two or three hours. I always read rapidly, easily grasping meanings and instantly retaining everything in mind. But that day, if I had been reading Spinoza instead of the Lana Turner interview it would have been the same: I understood nothing and I remembered nothing. And I would still like to learn something about Lana Turner . . .

I don't know how long it was after I had let the magazine fall from my hand, or how long it was after I had stretched my feet out on the desk and rested my head on the back of the armchair, but I fell into a deep sleep.

In my dream I saw a place where the floors and walls were covered with white tile. A scientist in a white jacket swung a test tube full of liquid back and forth in his hand and sang:

> Happy birthday, 478
> Happy birthday, 478
> Happy birthday, happy birthday
> Happy birthday, 478

In the corner, a messenger boy swung in a rocking chair, his feet unable to touch the floor.

"Nicholai!" he yelled, with the sourest face and in the most ill-tempered manner. "My name is Nicholai! Nicholai!" At that moment, someone dragged Esme along the floor while at the same time kicking her in the stomach. Monsieur Jacob emerged from a corner holding out to the scientist another full test tube; the two, arm in arm and bursting with laughter, launched into a cordial, even joyful, discussion. In order not to be seen I was squeezed into some corner, praying that they wouldn't notice me. Suddenly dozens of various kinds of birds dived in. The messenger boy, grabbing hold of their tails, began to fly. I couldn't contain myself any longer: "Nicholai! Don't leave me. Take me too, Nicholai!" I shouted, choking in a flood of tears.

I woke up in a sweat. It was long past midnight. I left the office building in a panic and ran straight for home.

It is hard for me to explain what happened next. Have you ever taken a beating at the hands of three total strangers? I did. Two of my teeth were knocked out; I had a black eye; every bone in my body ached for days, weeks; I couldn't have cared less. For that night, my pride was crushed: my precious honour that I had protected with my hermetic isolation, my savageness, my bull-headedness. If we were living in a Zen tale instead of real life, then I would have been awarded for my damaged pride without a doubt. In the end, the enlightenment and merit I'd achieved would be a golden crown on my head. But that isn't the case. At least it wasn't so for me.

Oh reader, that night while running straight for home my way was blocked by three people! And I was beaten to a pulp. I don't know who they were, I know nothing about them. I didn't look at their faces; I was ashamed to: ashamed both in their name and mine; ashamed in the name of that shitty situation and in the name of my anger, my hatred, and, more than anything else, my deep sorrow. But I am able to gather that they were the City Police, responsible for the city's common safety. In the course of being beaten, and unfortunately afterwards as well, various details remained nailed to my mind. For instance, they were dressed like this:

One of the men had on a pair of green and white striped trousers, a T-shirt with BUENOS AIRES IS COOL printed on it, a leather jacket, and a pair of army boots. His oily hair was tied back in a ponytail; in his ear there was a platinum earring in the shape of a dragon. The second man was baby-faced. His hair was cut short, the right side adorned with a blue wave. He wore a pair of tight jeans, a hooded grey sweatshirt, and a pair of sneakers. He smiled constantly while beating me and danced as if listening to some inaudible music. The woman was tall and broad. Her thick bleached-blonde hair stood on end. She wore tight leopard-print trousers, a black fishnet T-shirt, and a gold-coloured raincoat. On her feet she wore a pair of high-heeled patent leather boots. In one ear, she wore a Minnie Mouse earring, in the other a tiny diamond. Her long fingernails were painted gold. She was agile and struck hard. And she didn't break a nail either.

I closed myself up in my room at my mother's house. The days flowed past like a swollen, muddy river. I didn't go out of my room for exactly ten days. I tried to think of nothing; I read my horse trainer biography. On reaching the seventh volume, I was suddenly incredibly fed up. I couldn't root out the messenger boy murders from my soul no matter how hard I tried. What right had that city to burden me with such a mission? The City Council, the City Doctor, the City Police – the City's Messenger Boy Institution and the succession of murders – they were all inextricably linked! Having to meet new people in that city where I knew no one other than my mother, Wang Yu, and Monsieur Jacob; to be dragged from place to place as events unfolded; and as a finale, to be given a grand beating – I hated that city. I also hated my feverish young soul and its fits of curiosity.

I decided to leave on the first ship to embark from the port. My mother behaved as she did on every other departure: she cried and wouldn't speak to me. Wang Yu prepared a lovely picnic basket. I don't like farewells and greetings at all, but Wang Yu insisted so much on accompanying me to the port that I accepted.

"So long," he said, shaking my hand. "I will miss you."

I couldn't believe my ears. "Me?" I asked.

"You have your good points," he said.

"Thank you, Wang Yu," I said.

"I want to give you a going-away present," he said. He took something out of his pocket and handed it over. It was a pebble. "That was the only thing I took with me from India," he said, "and I've carried it at my side until the day I found someone worthy of it. You are well intentioned. You're brave hearted. Moreover, however rarely, you sometimes remind me of your grandfather."

"Where's this pebble from?"" I asked. "From Bombay?"

"That's not a pebble," said Wang Yu with a smile that resembled my mother's very much. "That is the kidney stone of the hijra leader who kidnapped me. While passing it he suffered so much that I've kept it as a memento of the most precious memory of my life."

I was speechless. I said goodbye quickly and climbed the gangway of the ship. After throwing my bag in my cabin, I went up on deck. I pitched Wang Yu's gift into the sea. Believe me, it's no small thing to rid yourself of the gift of a kidney stone.

For the first few days of the voyage I didn't leave my cabin very often. I read the seventh volume of the horse trainer biography. Even the most extensive biographies do not go beyond seven volumes. So when I finished my biography, I was obliged to join the life on the ship. I was sitting on one of the deckchairs arranged in rows and trying hard to focus on the surroundings, the sky (it was quite a demanding job for me), when a child drew my attention. He was a puny little thing. About six or seven years old. On his behind hung a pair of filthy bermuda shorts; on his feet a pair of navy blue canvas shoes; and hanging from his thin frame was a huge black T-shirt. With his back turned to me, he was leaning on the railing looking out at the sea. Oh reader, written on his T-shirt was this:

YOUR VIEW OF SOCIETY
SCREWS UP MY MIND
LIKE YOU WILL
NEVER KNOW

The child turned his face. It was Esme's son. I felt my knees shaking. His brilliant blue eyes met mine. Not only his clothes, but his face and body were also covered with grime. He smiled. He began walking towards me.

"Hello!" he said. His voice was bubbling over.

"Hel-hello, I mean, good day to you, messenger boy," I said.

"But I have a name," he said. He giggled.

"What's your name," I asked.

"Sebastian!" he told me.

Of course, Sebastian.

"Your mother – isn't your mother here?" I asked.

"Esme missed the boat," he said. "She went to see Uncle Domanya. She told me that if she missed the boat she'd board at a later port. So, I boarded. Our cabin is very nice; it's in C. And what about yours; where is it?" Not the slightest trace of the messenger boy remained. He was Esme's son.

"What's that writing on your back?" I asked.

"It's Cockney Rebel," he said. "It's a line from the song *Sebastian*. My mother was very pleased to find out my name was Sebastian. That's her favourite song. I had that line from the song printed on my T-shirt – nice, isn't it?"

"So, does that mean you chose your name because of that song?" I asked.

"Nooo, I chose it because it was Bach's name," he said. "Now I'm fed up with it, now I'd like another name instead. I'd like either Johann or Felix."

"Johann because of Bach again?" I queried.

"Yes, yes – I adore Bach," he said.

"But Felix is a cat's name," I said.

"What difference does it make?" he said.

That is true. What difference did it make? Johann or Felix!

He interjected merrily: "But my mother would like me to be called Teddy. Because of a story by Salinger. He is one of my mother's favourite writers. Did you know my mother's name is also from a Salinger story?"

"I didn't know that," I said. A lump came and settled in my throat. I felt like I was going to cry. I missed Esme so much. "I thought Professor Domanya gave her that name. He's your mother's godfather, you know."

"I don't think so actually," he said. He was so cheerful!

"You don't think so?" I said. At this point I couldn't keep my voice from shaking.

"My mother was born in India. She was raised there until the age of seven. Her father was an atheist, her mother apparently a Buddhist. Question One: why would they have her baptised? Two: Professor Domanya has never in his life been to India. In my opinion that is just an invention of Professor Domanya and my mother; it's not something I take seriously."

"I take it seriously!" I screamed. My voice had cracked. How quickly I became an ugly, vulgar person. My face had become red, my head jutted out in front of me. I had utterly disgraced myself in front of this small child.

"I love those seashells you gave me so much," he said. "They're always with me. You were right — whenever I'm down, they do the trick. Everyone adored them that night I returned from your place. I gave a few of them to my friends."

"Messenger boys?" I shouted in astonishment. Can't you even control your voice?! I had an incredible desire for a drink.

"Of course, who else?" he said. He winked.

Well, in this world where messenger boys could so easily transform into the most natural, easy-going children, it seems I couldn't manage to do anything but stutter and splutter, get angry and choke, shout and bluster.

"The murders — you know I didn't solve the murders," I said.

"There was nothing to solve anyway," he said. "We were committing suicide."

"You were committing suicide?" I was about to faint.

"Every one was a suicide in the guise of a murder," he said. "Those that wanted to die killed themselves one by one — and the rest of us, we created an aura of murder. We had decided on all of this beforehand."

"Why were you killing yourselves, dear child?" I demanded. "Why? Why?"

"Do you think our world is a good one?" he asked. His huge blue eyes locked onto mine. "We were aware of so much. We were fed up with being messenger boys, of that life, and we were killing ourselves from boredom. If my mother hadn't come and got me, I would be in the waiting line. And at the twelfth murder, you would have been dealing with my corpse. You know those injections they give us — the injections that insure we remain as messenger boys — even with these we could only live to the age of thirty at most. But once we stop them . . . "

"Stop them?"

"I think we'll be dead in one or two years. So, we would either have to stay as messenger boys until the end — or we could live one or two years as children. Of course that wouldn't be possible in the city. But Esme made my choice possible. I'll live for one or two years as a child — what do say to that?"

"Have you stopped taking your injections?" I asked. I was filled with horror.

"The injections are a monopoly of the City Council," he said. "The price of being a messenger boy. Don't you understand — I was going to kill myself rather than remain a messenger boy. I don't want to live longer than two years anyway. Whether as a boy or a messenger boy, life is too tedious."

"So it was the Messenger Boy Suicides, then?" I said. "That's what it was?"

"Uh-huh," he said. "Isn't that something?"

"Quite something!" I said. "So is it still going on?"

"Uh-huh," he said. "Last night another one of us killed himself. I believe we are going to put an end to that precious institution. One of our aims was this: to stop them from producing messenger boys."

"Did Monsieur Jacob know this?" I asked.

He burst into laughter. "I won't tell!" he shouted. Tears of laughter poured from his eyes.

"Why me?" I asked.

"I won't tell!" he said. He skipped away.

Other translated fiction by Milet:

The Other Side of the Mountain
Erendiz Atasü
Translated by Erendiz Atasü & Elizabeth Maslen

A Cup of Turkish Coffee
Buket Uzuner
Translated by Pelin Arıner

Fourth Company
Rıfat Ilgaz
Translated by Damian Croft

Out of the Way! Socialism's Coming!
Aziz Nesin
Translated by Damian Croft

Radical Niyazi Bey
Muzaffer İzgü
Translated by Damian Croft

A Summer Full of Love
Füruzan
Translated by Damian Croft